ATROPOS PRESS
new york • dresden

Hospitality in the age of media representation

Christian Hänggi

© 2009 by Christian Hänggi

Think Media EGS Series is supported by the European Graduate School

ATROPOS PRESS
New York • Dresden

US: 151 First Avenue # 14, New York, N.Y. 10003
Germany: Mockritzer Str. 6, D-01219 Dresden

cover design: Hannes Charen

ISBN 978-0-9748534-6-8

Contents

Preface   9

1   **Advertising: a mental institution**   15
1.1   Self-cannibalisation of advertising   15
1.2   The con/fusion of natural and legal persons   21
1.3   Communication as information transmission   33
1.4   The disappearance of critical distance   37
1.5   The price of communication   44
1.6   Conclusion   49

2   **Communication as being-with-others**   51
2.1   Etymological considerations   51
2.2   The gift of communication   53
2.2.1   Question and answer   55
2.2.2   Deferring the decision   58
2.2.3   The gift of marriage   61
2.3   The habitual   64
2.4   Issues of friendship   65
2.4.1   Usefulness   67
2.4.2   Pleasure   70
2.4.3   I, Thou, and being-with   72
2.5   Conclusion   77

3   **Communication as life**   79
3.1   Zoé and bios   80
3.2   Between birth and death   86
3.3   Ambiguities in artificial life   91
3.4   Balance as the paradigm of communication   96

4	**Economy: sharing the home**	105
4.1	Hospitality	107
4.1.1	The questions of the host and the foreigner	110
4.1.2	The rules of the sovereign	114
4.1.3	The threshold	118
4.1.4	Filtering	124
4.2	Architectures of the home	128
4.2.2	The castle	131
4.2.3	The home without walls	133
4.2.4	The windowless monad	137
4.2.5	Conclusion	141
4.3	The disappearing sovereign	142
5	**The challenge of productivity**	147
5.1	Unproductivity as the mode of economy	150
5.2	Generating life	154
5.3	Sustainability: the ecology of the mind	157
6	**The self and its brain**	161
6.1	Brain, mind, consciousness	162
6.2	Plasticity and flexibility	164
6.3	The plasticities of the brain	167
7	**Towards responsiveness in and in confrontation of advertising**	173
	Acknowledgments	183
	Bibliography	185

Preface

Advertising beleaguers the lives we live. The economic sector employs an enormous ensemble of strategies and tactics to direct our attention to its commodities, whether we want or not. The bulk of media is made in such a way that it can never know whether we pay attention to it. It can therefore not cater to our individual | *not so any more* needs and wants, and it does not register when we would rather be left alone. The advertising industry meets this problem with more advertising, leading to a veritable economy of excess.

But what exactly is the problem with advertising? On the one hand, there are subjective problems, namely that most advertising is banal and aesthetically hideous on the level of content and design. There are also objective problems: advertising gets into our way but does not carry information that can justly be considered valuable; it does not meet our wishes; it thinks only in economic terms, never in societal or political terms; and it promotes such thinking and is even capable of forcing the mass media to make concessions. When a major bank commissions an ad every time a newspaper reports on a regatta, this alone is a good reason to report on that regatta. When a beverage manufacturer pays for the entire sports equipment of a high school, it may be considered coherent that this school bans apparel with the competitor's logo. When an outdoor advertiser gives money to a city to post billboards, this money is a good enough reason to blindly accept the deal. When the political sector tries to confine advertising, the advertising sector immediately starts a lament on the violation of economic freedom if not freedom of expression. In brief: advertising cements an image of societal life that no longer exists, an image that is detrimental to the singular person, the civil society and the freedom of information.

The book at hand developed from my dissertation *Hospitality in the age of media representation*. My doctoral advisor Wolfgang Schirmacher once said that I was explaining advertising through philosophy and philosophy through advertising. I tend to agree even though I am not entirely sure if that is philosophy. What I dare claim with some certainty is that thinking about the role of advertising in our society and—more importantly—in our singular lives, is currently at a regrettable low. The industry discourse is a discourse *within* advertising instead of *on* advertising. The intertrade organisations are dominated by practitioners that are about to be retired soon and that are affiliated with each other to such an extent that critical thinking can be excluded from the start. The mass media live on advertising and disregard the issue almost completely. The political sector is only interested in advertising when it carries content that is objected to on moral grounds. Even philosophy currently does not present a comprehensive vision on advertising. It seems too worldly for a serious investigation. The advertising critique that had a brief heyday around the turn of the millennium did not so much discuss advertising in itself as the content it transports and the way of life it promotes in the eyes of the critics.

Despite the lack of an overall vision, we can find striking thoughts offering us unexpected insights in contemporary philosophy, but also in biology, semiotics, neurology, literature and economic theory. With a little bit of patience, they beautifully combine to a more comprehensive picture that, I believe, shows us why the phenomenon of advertising deserves our attention. This book contrasts the self-image of the responsible citizen with the self-image of advertising and asks what claims advertising that is programmed to merely send can make on our attention.

The first chapter is dedicated to advertising and clarifying some terms. It discusses character traits of advertising whose understanding is of importance for the development of the argument. When looking at the discourses within the industry and the mission statements of inter-trade organisations, it becomes evident that it is not clear, who advertising actually addresses. Sometimes it is supposed to address the consumer, sometimes the citizen. There is an apparent confusion of the terms, which leads to a dilution of the societal claims the advertising industry makes. In this chapter, I observe an understanding of communication as something which is not circular, something that can be reduced to mere information transmission. Lastly, I try to address the question whether advertising causes a lack of critical distance, thus a lack of an impartial view on the phenomenon.

The second chapter attends to the question of communication. It asks whether communication requires circularity and circulation, in other words, whether it requires the possibility of an answer. The ruminations make use of the idea of the gift and the countergift which exhibits a similar problem structure when contrasting different thinkers. It turns out that a decision on this problem does not do justice to it, which in no way diminishes the urgency of an answer. I go on to imagining that the communicators are linked by a bond of friendship because different types of friendship area also based on mutuality or one-sidedness. What this leads to is the question whether communication is being-with-others or being-for-others and I notice that the former names the infrastructure, the interrelatedness of everything, while the latter brings in an ethical dimension that is guided by love.

This interrelatedness is also the basis for the considerations in the third chapter, "Communication as life". The Greek *zoé* designated the fact of bare life while *bios* meant life in society. Here again, we can make out a similar pattern. First, life for the sake of life must be guaranteed. Only then can we bring in a prescriptive or ethical component. Natural life takes place between birth and death, but also between death and birth and mankind is part of the history of nature. When we think about life, but also about advertising, we cannot refrain from asking what artificial life is, that is, life born from human technology. It turns out that the concept of artificial life also comes with some contradictions. The symbol of the balance illustrates that these contradictions are not to be cancelled out but must haggle forever with each other in a constant dialogue that cannot stop if it is not to solidify into inertia.

The fourth chapter is the central chapter of this attempt to discuss whether the idea of hospitality is suited for understanding our relationship with advertising. This is not so far-fetched a hypothesis considering that economy essentially means the sharing of the house. We can read this "sharing of the house" literally and ask ourselves, who we want to share our house with and under what conditions. This book however goes further and proposes that our mind, that is, the mental capacity the advertising industry is aiming at, also faces this problem. After the cultural and economic undermining of the role of the sovereign of the house, what is left is our mind that we want to freely dispose of. Under what conditions do we let the foreign, that is, advertising, let take part in our mind? We develop filters that take on the task of deciding automatically, at least in parts. Filters based on empirical value are however often unsatisfactory mechanisms to do justice to the question of friend and foe. Our senses also act as filters for our brain, which leads us to considerations of the monad. The monad is the smallest, indivisible entity that is connected to other monads in a prestabilised harmony. We can image the monad as a house where the windows of our senses on the ground floor absorb the environment and pass it on to the second floor, where the soul dwells.

When we speak of economy and when we face the exuberance that nature bestows on us, we are already in the middle of the questions of productivity. In the fifth chapter I propose to replace the term productivity, which is always goal-oriented, with the term generativity. Generativity is in the realm of a kind of thinking that frees that which we generate. This chapter also treats questions of ecology and sustainability, because if we want to come to a "good" relationship with advertising, we must be sure that this relationship leaves space for the care of current and the creation of future life. We want to be capable of offering hospitality in our minds not only today but also tomorrow.

After I opened the focus on the ecosystem, I bring biology back to the microsystem of our brain. In the sixth chapter I observe how the terms brain, mind and consciousness have different meanings in our language but imply each other and are often used synonymously. What this really boils down to is that we acquire a consciousness of our brain, a kind of self-awareness that is practiced as an exercise in plasticity. The brain is a plastic organ, which on the one hand means it is able to be formed, an ability that is today celebrated under the idea of flexibility. On the other hand, it means that this organ is able to form itself and in a second instance the environment that surrounds it, which in an endless feedback loop again forms the brain.

What does this all mean for our confrontation with advertising? The last chapter brings the different viewpoints together and advocates an active participation in shaping our environment. This participation grounds on a sense of responsibility and interrelatedness.

So much for the overview. The really exciting insights are however not synthesised in these few paragraphs. They are scattered throughout the book, sometimes in inconspicuous relative clauses, sometimes as grand topics that turn up again and again. I allow myself excursions to literature, biosemiotics, human rights. I let an advertiser speak, go over to a philosopher, have Pippi Longstocking meet Zarathustra. And always with my mind on what the findings might teach us about the being of advertising and whether it allows us to draw any conclusions as to how we are to deal with it.

1 Advertising: a mental institution

1.1 Self-cannibalisation of advertising

"Formerly one wanted to be 'talked' about; that is no longer enough, since the market has grown too large—only a 'shout' will do."[1] We have little idea of the sensorial reality of the days when Friedrich Nietzsche's *Gay Science* was first published in 1882. As a man of poor eyesight, he was extraordinarily sensitive to his aural environment and treated hearing as a sense superior to vision. We may assume that technology has brought about changes which have increased the overall noise level since those days: cars, airplanes, streetcars on the one hand; devices to reproduce music and speech and to distribute them across the land on the other hand.

At the same time, improvements in reproductive techniques in the visual field, such as print and paint technologies and desktop publishing, have led to a considerable increase in visual stimuli: our environment bears witness to a veritable "colour explosion", as Vilém Flusser observes when he compares the visual environment of communist Eastern Europe and the West.[2] The general availability of electricity and means of transportation have opened new physical and mental environments and further confused

---

1   Nietzsche, Gay Science, §331.
2   Flusser, Medienkultur, 2. *All non-English sources are translated by the author unless a translation is indicated in the bibliography.*

distinctions between public and private. The gradual disintegration of the authoritarian state in favour of a free market economy has led to an attitude in the economic sphere which considers it not only acceptable but desirable that a lack of financial state involvement in the public sector is made up for by advertising[3] and sponsorship.[4] Scientific advances are harnessed by the advertising industry to open up new sensorial experiences involving not only sounds and sights but also smells and tactile experiences. We are so deep inside the self-sufficient economic systems and the idea of progress that even when we project alternative worlds, such as Second Life, we project the same economic model of the world on a different physical scale without even noticing.[5]

Let us listen to Nietzsche again:

'Better deaf than deafened'—Formerly one wanted to be 'talked' about; that is no longer enough, since the market has grown too large—only a 'shout' will do. As a result, even good voices shout themselves down, and the best goods are offered by hoarse voices; without the vendors' cry and hoarseness there is no longer any genius. That is, to be sure, a bad epoch for a thinker; he must learn how to find his own quietude even between two noises, and pretend he is deaf until he really is. As long as he has not learned this, he runs the risk of going to pieces from impatience and headaches.[6]

---

3   "Advertising" or the "Advertising complex", formerly called "propaganda" or "publicity", is to be understood as the complex of disciplines active in the promotion of companies and their products and services: advertising, marketing, branding, public relations, investor relations, media relations, and many more.

4   See: Klein, No Logo.

5   Schirmacher observes: "The Internet increasingly offers a doubling of our familiar reality." Net Culture.

6   Nietzsche, Gay Science, §331.

Nietzsche retreats in order to avoid the vendors' cries, but the moment he is back to testify of his retreat, he will have to face the noise again, and chances are he is even more sensible to those cries after a period of quietude.

One might argue that the "best goods" (as Nietzsche calls them) offered deserve a louder, sharper voice to promote them so that they may stand out against merchandise of inferior quality. One might also argue that the best goods of the nineteenth century are inferior to those of the twenty-first century. It is however difficult to prove the marketed goods have in fact increased in quality.[7] Quality has little to do with advertising (as it has little to do with perception of quality, which is the very playground for advertising), so the qualitative argument is not valid for a justification of advertising.

Marshall McLuhan, well aware that the quality of a product is not decisive, notes that the advertising industry makes use of repetition to persuade those addressed: "Ads push the principle of noise all the way to the plateau of persuasion."[8] Since all advertising wants to persuade in some way and has to face trade rivalry, if one advertiser increases the level of stimuli, all others need to do likewise and will likely do so by use of repetition. This vicious circle of outdoing the competition defers the issue of the overall noise level,

7   It is problematic to compare the quality of a cart wheel of the nineteenth
     century to a car wheel of the twentieth century, a strawberry of the sixteenth
     century to one of the twenty-first century and so on. If quality means the
     lack of defective parts, then the comparison with modern technology is
     even more difficult. Modern products typically have more parts than ancient
     products and thus more parts that may become defective. As Anders claims
     many products today are produced in such a way that they will have to be
     replaced after a number of years have passed and thus keep the economic
     engine running (Anders, Die Antiquiertheit des Menschen, Band II, 15–16;
     38ff), while Braungart and McDonough observe that the industrial revolu-
     tion has brought us many products that are detrimental to nature and natural
     diversity of organisms and cultures (Braungart and McDonough, 38).
8   McLuhan, Understanding Media, 227.

since sensibility decreases with an increase in stimuli.[9] A decrease in sensibility results in a decrease of impact. Georg Felser refers to a number of studies and notes that more than 85% of advertising has no impact. Out of 1600 advertising messages, only 80 are consciously perceived and only 28 in a positive way.[10] Another study has revealed that no more than 5% of the advertising information reaches its addressees.[11] Yet another study claims consumers only processed 1% of advertising messages in 1991 whereas in the 1960s, they perceived about 30–40%.[12] Again, the decrease in sensibility is generally not met by a decrease in messages which would result in an increase in sensibility, but by a further increase in messages. Consequently, the credibility of advertising in the eyes of consumers has decreased over the years.[13]

This book will elaborate on a number of inconsistencies in the advertising practice in particular and in communications in general that prevent us from turning communication technology from tools or "extensions of man" into "life techniques" so as to adapt technology in the broadest sense to find a "way to naturally comply with the cosmos",[14] that is, to comply with the interrelatedness of everything and overcome instrumentalised technology and communications. It will attempt to find ways so as not to be deafened by the vendors' cries; ways not to even have to pretend to be deaf because "the phenomenon which lends itself to our interpretation requires the courage of the seeing and hearing person, who may not pretend to be blind or deaf."[15]

---

9   Felser, Werbe- und Konsumentenpsychologie, 71–73.
10   Ibid., 4.
11   Ibid.
12   Ibid.
13   Ibid.
14   Schirmacher, Ereignis Technik, 100.
15   Ibid., 15.

Most of the technological advances that have had an impact on society and society's singularities (formerly: "individuals") can be said to be communication technologies: from means of transportation of material goods, a point particularly stressed by Canadian thinkers such as Harold Innis, to electric and electronic means of transportation of immaterial goods. "Communication" has come to encompass the totality of human and non-human interactions, though the anthropocentric use of the word clearly dominates in everyday language.

The term "communication" originated in the sixteenth century[16] and has become an object of considerable interest only in the twentieth century. It has been increasingly adapted to suit a wide variety of uses in the biological, economical, technological, and philosophical fields, among many others. Along with the increasing use of the term we witness a quantitative growth and spread of communication acts in all these fields—and consequently an increase in communication acts in all available media—,an increase which directly aims at our mental sphere. With each new media technology, we sooner than later get a new wave of advertising occupying a large share of the information volume.[17] Most unasked-for messages can be traced back to commercial communications in some way, which is why this book focuses on the advertising complex. It can be argued whether most of these messages are really unasked-for. Günther Anders claims that advertising is superfluous in markets where the consumers cry for the

---

16   KLUGE Etymologisches Wörterbuch der deutschen Sprache (hereinafter: KLUGE), "Kommunikation".

17   Several researchers and critics have attempted to determine the number of commercial messages we are confronted with each day. These range from 1500 (Lasn, 1999, 292) and 3000 (American Association of Advertising Agencies, in Twitchell, 1996, 3, and Hayden, 2001) to as high as 15 000 (Berger, 2000, 81) and 16 000 (Savan, 1994, 1). According to the Symantec Internet Security Threat Report, between 1 July and 31 December 2006, spam made up 59% of all monitored email traffic.

goods and not vice versa.[18] Thus, in markets with heavy competition and low interest of consumers for products, advertising needs to address all those whose interest is low and must be persuaded or encouraged to need a particular product. The vendor's voices get hoarser and consequently less productive. The thinker's challenge to withdraw becomes more difficult to accomplish.

The idea of advertising has become internalised in the idea of a free market to such an extent that it is no longer a question whether to do advertising—and often not even *how* to do it. Commercial communications claim that the free market economy comes with a right of "freedom of expression", which generally allows any kind of promotion anywhere and at any time. This claim is based on the wrong premises since in reality neither the market economy nor freedom of speech is in fact free because there are too many conflicting interests involved. Advertising has come to a stall where its most potent enemy is self-cannibalisation and its productivity in the economic or creative sense has to be questioned not so much in order to help the advertising industry gain some sort of allegedly lost credibility[19] but in order to project and realise an environment, which reclaims fields for a freedom of thought in a manner that leaves room for the ability to meet present needs without compromising those of future generations.

There are a number of paradigms in the economic sector in general, and in advertising in particular, that have led to an instrumental view of communication: the blurring distinction between natural persons and legal persons; the idea of communication as mere one-way information transmission; the loss of critical distance; and the attribution of monetary values to communication acts.

---

18   Anders, Die Antiquiertheit des Menschen, Band II, 313.
19   See: Felser, Werbe- und Konsumentenpsychologie, 2.

1.2   The con/fusion of natural and legal persons

The first paradigm of an instrumental view of communication originated with the distinction between "natural person" and "legal person". At first it appears as if sufficient similarities can be observed between corporations and people to justify the designation of "person" for both entities. Hügli and Lübcke define "person" as a "subject, insofar as it owns, apart from a consciousness, a body, a recognisable and active relationship to its environment (i.e. also to other persons) and an individual history, thanks to which the individual in question develops certain assets, attitudes, character traits and opinions on itself and the world."[20] If we accept that a body is made up of multiple bodies of another order (such as the company's body is made up of human bodies) and that this body can have a consciousness, we should have little difficulty in accepting the term "person" for both entities. Disciplines such as branding make sure that attitudes and character traits are streamlined within an enterprise with respect to that enterprise and its environment so that we can speak of a corporate identity. (Notice how *corpus*, body, is the root of words such as corporation and corporate and how "body" is used to designate a singular body as well as a body of bodies.)

> A corporation is an artificial being, invisible, intangible, and existing
> only in contemplation of law. Being the mere creature of law, it pos-
> sesses only those properties which the charter of its creation confers
> upon it […] Among the most important are immortality, and, if the
> expression may be allowed, individuality […] A perpetual succes-
> sion of individuals are capable of acting for the promotion of the
> particular object, like one immortal being.[21]

---

20   Hügli & Lübcke, "Person".
21   Chief Justice Marshall, in: Richard Powers, "An Artificial Being". In: Latour &

Conferring the status of "person" both to humans and to companies gives them rights and obligations—but at different scales and rhythms. The distinction between natural and legal persons is a legal construct, which must be reviewed in the light of its actual workings—a task which this book will only briefly touch upon. Sam Weber reminds us that Carl Schmitt viewed a legal person as a "mode of calculation"[22] but then unfortunately went on to define a "person" as "its ability to be elsewhere and other and yet at the same time remain itself."[23] This definition is adept to describe a legal person understood as a body with multiple bodies who all stand for the single corporate body but need not be in one place at one time, but it is not able to define a natural person in the traditional sense.[24] Only organisations (corporations, church, states) used to represent themselves independent of time and place and act around the clock in the same name and as the same body.

When a natural person utilises the field of opportunities opened by technological developments in the communication sector and transcends the biological body, as is the case with people in the spotlight of media, he or she becomes something like a legal person in his or her own right and loses—in Walter Benjamin's terms—his or her aura. The biological, perishable body stops existing on a billboard or on TV.[25] In the 1994 introduction to McLuhan's Understanding Media, Lewis H. Lapham makes a similar observation with reference to death: "[O]n the smooth surfaces of the magazines the faces look as vacant and as imperturbable

---

Weibel (Eds.), Making Things Public: Atmospheres of Democracy, 614.

22   Weber, Targets of Opportunity, 32.

23   Ibid., 38.

24   There has been some change in this with media that enable us to communicate even if we are physically present elsewhere. However, there is still only one natural body to communicate.

25   It must be noted though that such media may—after the perishing of who is represented—also serve as a "cult of remembrance of loved ones" (Benjamin, Illuminations, 226).

as they have looked for twenty years [...] Like minor deities, [celebrities] ease the pain of doubt and hold at bay the fear of death."[26] This lack of perspective on the other's death—which, to follow Emmanuel Levinas, is the first death—sheds a different light on one's own death and may deprive us of a certain sensibility of running forward to our own death, come back and frame our lives and our responsibility with respect to the knowledge of our death. Before the advent of organised civilisation with multi-bodied entities transcending the biological lifespan of its constituents, only the Gods were considered immortal and, consequently, only Gods were omniscient. Paul Virilio not only makes a point in that the attributes of God are ubiquity, immediacy and instantaneity; he also observes that the humans who dispose of these attributes are becoming the new monarchs.[27] He explicitly refers to how Silvio Berlusconi is "telepresent" when he is absent, that his telegenius constantly makes sure that he is simultaneously here and elsewhere—in other words: nowhere.[28]

Unlike the Christian God, multi-bodied entities and overdetermined mediated persons do not enter into a singular relationship with human singularities: "Instead of presenting a private argument or vista, [advertising] offers a way of life that is for everybody or nobody."[29] The sense of being nowhere by being everywhere can be attributed to the fact that there is only one biological body and the representations thereof are mediatised images or simulacra of that body. On the level of information technology, the biological body vanishes because the information density is reduced for the transmission of information—from 3D to 2D, from an intensive

26   Lapham, in: McLuhan, Understanding Media, xx.
27   Virilio, Seminar at the European Graduate School in La Rochelle, France. 30
        March 2007. See also: Virilio, Ereignislandschaft, 54.
28   Virilio, Ereignislandschaft, 32.
29   McLuhan, Understanding Media, 230f.

body to a representation at 72, 300, 600 dots per inch.[30] The loss of aura can be attributed to *overdetermination* and the *exchangeability* of media content.

Overdetermination can be understood as the multiple forces active at once in a situation. Overdetermination in our context can be understood as the process in which a number of people produce a saturated piece of information, which is then fed to a receiver with imaginary attributes. McLuhan comments that "[f]ar more thought and care go into the composition of any prominent ad in a newspaper or magazine than go into the writing of their features or editorials."[31] There is a narrow gap or none at all which involves the receiver in a creative or sensual process to determine a meaning which differs from the obvious one or to play with several meanings, very much in the way Roland Barthes states in his essay "Striptease" that "woman is desexualised at the very moment when she is stripped naked."[32] When she is desexualised she is deprived of the sex, of the reproductive, generative organ. In the overdetermined piece of information, the biological, reproductive body vanishes because the communication act is stripped of all natural occurrences, all flaws, inconsistencies and recurrence to a breathing subject: "By unveiling everything, [inauthentic dissimulation] hides that whose essence resides in its remaining hidden, namely, the authentic mystery of the person."[33]

What lies at the core of all advertising is a simple command "look at me", or rather "perceive me" or "pay attention to me". The advertising man Howard L. Gossage, who is credited for having

---

30   Cloning opens a new chapter in this respect since it allows to reproduce a physical body in such a way that it is in perceptively identical to the original. There is a qualitative shift in that the information is no longer a piece of information, a selection of certain representable attributes, but the thing itself.

31   McLuhan, Understanding Media, 228.

32   Barthes, Mythologies, 84.

33   Derrida, The Gift of Death, 37.

introduced McLuhan to the United States,[34] observed in an essay on billboards, that advertising sells something it doesn't own,
namely one's field of vision.[35] In general we can say advertising
sells people's field of perception. Felser does not jump to the selling
aspect when he argues that the functions of advertising are to inform, to motivate, to socialise, to amplify and to entertain.[36] These
are however only secondary functions of advertising. Information,
motivation, socialisation, amplification and entertainment are to
be read with respect to and in the internal logic of the advertised
product. The function is not to inform the society about whatever, but about what is advertised. David Ogilvy, founder of one
of the largest advertising agencies in the world, contests some of
Felser's points saying that, for him, "advertising is neither a form
of art nor of entertainment but an information medium. And I do
not want that you find one of my advertisements 'creative' but that
you find it so interesting that you *buy the product.*"[37] The ultimate goal is thus to get the receiver of the piece of information to
buy the advertised product or service; all the other functions can
be considered secondary functions, or rather, strategies that are
expected to lead to this goal. Thus, even if advertising deliberately
constructs gaps to be filled by the receiver to achieve a higher involvement, it is *overdetermined on the level of possible responses.*
The only feedback mechanism intrinsic to advertising is a binary
code "buy/not buy". Other responses may be called for (such as

34 Gossage, The Book of Gossage ("McLuhan would later say that Howard
    was one of the first people in the world to understand the point of his book
    [Understanding Media]. As soon as Howard figured it out, he explained
    to McLuhan what he, McLuhan, was trying to say." [41–42]). See also:
    "Understanding Marshall McLuhan", 242.
35 Gossage, The Book of Gossage, 113. In general we can say advertising sells
    people's field of perception.
36 Felser, Werbe- und Konsumentenpsychologie, 6.
37 Ogilvy, Über Werbung, 7. Similarly, Tages-Anzeiger quotes Peter Felser, the
    Swiss ad man of the year 2007: "Werbung muss verkaufen. Sonst nichts."
    (Advertising has to sell. Nothing else.) (Tages-Anzeiger, 18 Jan 2007).

"pleasing/displeasing" or the hypothetical "would you buy/would you not buy?"), but in the end, all lead up to the long-term success of the company, which is usually established by an optimal sale of products and services. The company is interested in responses only as long as they in some way further the sales.

Exchangeability on the other hand implies a certain irrelevance—understood as the negation of relevance, not its denial.[38] We can speak of irrelevance because the content can be replaced by an endless number of other content due to large-scale reproduction and the unending stream of new information items that enjoy more actuality. Exchangeability is the reason Jacques Derrida can maintain that "[t]echnological civilization only produces a heightening or recrudescence of the orgiastic [...] to the extent that it also produces boredom, for it 'levels' or neutralizes the mysterious or irreplaceable uniqueness of the responsible self."[39] Exchangeability forks into *reproducibility* and *functional exchangeability*. Like overdetermination, exchangeability is characterised by a certain lack of a biological singularity as outlined above, a lack of aura,[40] which brings us back to some considerations on time and place, whose transcendence we claimed above is only available to legal persons. Aura implies a certain time and place, which also implies the departure from that time and place.[41] It is a way of experiencing, of perceiving rather than a characteristic of the artwork.[42] Thus, we are urged to think of overdetermination and exchangeability in terms of degrees and are reminded that it is not only the medium itself which defines the message. A movie may be more or less overdetermined in its meanings and an advertisement may be

---

38   A mass-reproduced piece of information may gain relevance because it becomes part of the public discourse, but it is replaceable nonetheless.
39   Derrida, The Gift of Death, 36.
40   Benjamin, The Work of Art in the Age of Mechanical Reproduction.
41   Weber in Ferris, Walter Benjamin: Theoretical Questions, 35.
42   Ferris, Walter Benjamin: Theoretical Questions, 21.

deliberately constructed as underdetermined to achieve a deeper involvement. The exchangeability of certain works may very well contribute to an aura if we are prepared to let go and replace them with new ones, that is, if we are prepared to depart from the time and place of the artwork. We talk about the aura of the perishable in this context, an attitude which takes us forward to death, to the cult of remembrance. At the same time, the reproduction of works of art, as it was cultivated by artists as early as Edvard Munch as part of the creative or commercial process, may also lend a kind of aura to an artwork. As Anders argues, we make serial products retroactively auratic, we "soak them with our Daseins atmosphere."[43]

If the output of the advertising complex is exchangeable, there must be something which is constant so as to set in relation to this exchangeability. The constant is in fact the overdetermination and the exchangeability itself, just like biological bodies differ in that they are different. It is perhaps in this that we can again reconcile certain notions of biological bodies and artificial organisations under the notion of "person".

Biological bodies may also be exchangeable or irrelevant to other biological bodies but this exchangeability takes place in the area of interest or function and not in the area of reproducibility. When natural persons reproduce, this does not take place in the realm of production but in the realm of generation. This reproductive process is not a genetically identical reproduction but a reproduction or generation of something which is endowed with an inherent capacity to independently reproduce in turn. The functional exchangeability is most evident at the level of organisations where one functional body can be replaced by another body fulfilling the same function or—on a more personal level—by the replacement of friends or lovers by others. This is also the case

---

43   Anders, Die Antiquiertheit des Menschen, Band II, 44.

with advertising. Potential consumers can be replaced by others if they refuse to consume.

As was said before, legal persons are artificial constructs, bodies, made up of many acting bodies they could not act without, very much like the human body is a natural body made up of many independent yet correlated bodies (organs, cells, bacteria) it could not act without. Legal persons are not subject to the same combustive cycles as natural persons, something we intuitively know but fail to be conscious of when equalling the status of natural person to that of legal person.

We can understand the human being as the hypocenter of human communications, the site directly below, above, or at the point of an outbreak, an eruption or explosion. If the human body is the hypocenter—the eruption of a second order, near the site where the explosion occurs but never identical with it—it is his organs that make up the first order.[44] Many such second-order-bodies make up the body of a legal person who—thanks to intra-organisational functional exchangeability—never sleeps, never eats and only rarely copulates.[45] The main challenge which arises in external communications of a corporate body is paradoxically that, in reference to Virilio, "talking" to an enterprise, one feels there is no one there because there is always someone there.[46] At the same time, each human body involved in the corporate body knows the makeup of the organisation allows that he or she can go

44   This chain of orders of eruption can be traced down even further: if organs are the first order, synapses may be considered the zero order. The chapter "The self and its brain" will dedicate more thought to the brain.

45   This legal body—in today's practice—cannot be appropriately likened to Abraham Bosse's creature on the frontispiece of Hobbes' Leviathan since many enterprises today are not ruled by an absolute sovereign but organised in flat hierarchies or matrices of hierarchies. Interestingly, the general assembly, the management and the governing board of a company are called the "organs".

46   Virilio, Ereignislandschaft, 32.

on leave or quit the job without causing major malfunctioning to or discontinuation of the corporate body, unlike our organs which cannot stop working without ultimately killing off the body with its other organs and thus making it impossible to reintroduce that rebelling organ's activity at a later point in time.

Natural persons working for legal persons never speak for themselves (if they do their job the way they are expected to) but someone or something else, namely the artificial construct of the enterprise. Who speaks and who is spoken for is never identical and this poses a great challenge for the issue of responsibility. In Nietzsche's days, the market vendor or the salesman may have been identical with the enterprise, and if they were not, they were at least a singular human to take recourse to and who had to answer before the addressee they were trying to convince of their merchandise. McLuhan locates the disappearance of the salesman in the era of Arthur Miller's *Death of a Salesman* and observes how he has been replaced by more complex constructs: "The simple faith of the salesman in the irresistibility of his line (both talk and goods) now yields to the complex togetherness of the corporate posture, the process and the organization."[47] Or in Lapham's words, in the introduction to *Understanding Media*: "The individual voice and singular point of view disappears into the chorus of a corporate and collective consciousness."[48] When too many speak through a single channel or message and both the singular point of view as well as the singular human being vanish, then there is no one to take full responsibility. Responsibility may also be shared, but shared responsibility is not multiplied but partial, thus mutilated, and consequently not the ethical answer to the encounter with singularities.

---

47   McLuhan, Understanding Media, 232.
48   Lapham, in: McLuhan, Understanding Media, xxi.

We may say that any body of multiple bodies is a *Limited Inc.*, a *Société à responsabilité limitée.*[49] It is interesting to observe that the term *"Limited Inc."* does not state what it is that is limited (though we could read it as a limitation on the degree of incorporation, of putting in bodies, of including), while its French equivalent, *Sarl*, clearly states that what is limited is responsibility. The German equivalent, *Gesellschaft mit beschränkter Haftung, GmbH,* offers yet another reading: in German it is not so much responsibility, that is, a certain burden assumed projecting one's acts into the future, which is limited, but *Haftung*, accountability or liability, that is, a responsibility towards something that has already taken place and was somehow—at least partially—caused by that *Gesellschaft.* A question that arises here is the difference between the society with limited responsibility/accountability and the other society. Does the existence of the terms *Sarl* and *GmbH* indicate that there is such a society, a community, the community of mankind perhaps, which assumes full responsibility? Or is it trying to suggest there are other commercial "societies", the *Aktiengesellschaft, AG,* for instance, the stock corporation, incorporated company or public company, that assume full responsibility? As long as we speak German or Italian *(società per azioni, s.p.a.)* we are tempted to believe this since it is the shares *(Aktien, azioni)* that represent the corporation. But again, the *Aktiengesellschaft* only assumes responsibility to the extent that the shareholder equity can cover it. The stock exchange value of the shares is a form of representation and subject to fluctuation. The second trap in this reading lies in introducing a net difference between GmbH and AG. The type of responsibility or liability they assume is more or less the same and may de facto only differ in the share equity. The literal reading of the French equivalent to *Aktiengesellschaft* somehow repeats the insight of *société à responsabilité limitée,* but makes a clearer statement

---

49   See also: Derrida, LIMITED INC a b c..., 63.

as to the form of the society: *société anonyme (SA)*. An SA is not anonymous in itself, and its shareholders are not necessarily anonymous, but accountability/liability is chopped up in such a way that only an anonymous, amorphous construct may be called on. Even if members of the board of directors or the management may be held accountable and sentenced, they remain mediated representatives of the corporation and not necessarily human beings that are driven by a personal sense of responsibility.

∞ Insert: Art and advertising

We will spend a few thoughts on art and advertising since their creation is largely identical at the technical level. Even though we should refrain from drawing a clear demarcation line between works of art and advertising and instead think in degrees, there are some differences that can be made out at the polar ends of this confrontation.

Works of art generally satisfy a need (that of the creator and that of the spectator) while advertising generally triggers a need. The spectator, or: the *host* of the artwork or the piece of advertising, is not aware beforehand which need is evoked or satisfied. Although the needs—and consequently their satisfaction or evocation—are only triggered upon reception of the information (upon reception of the *foreigner*), there is a difference in the mindset of the receiver (host). Intuitively, we know if something is art or advertising and it is surprising that many of those who most vehemently support advertising in public space are the harshest critics of art and "bad" architecture in public space.

In advertising we receive in a state of distraction and in art we receive in a state of concentration—a distinction Benjamin makes

between works with and works without an aura.[50] Martin Buber
writes: "The essential deed of art determines the process whereby
the form becomes a work. That which confronts me is fulfilled
through the encounter through which it enters into the world of
things in order to remain incessantly effective, incessantly It—but
also infinitely able to become again a You, enchanting and inspir-
ing."[51] Expressed on a different gradual axis, we dare to state that
artwork is consumed by virtue of our decision while advertising is
consumed by virtue of someone else's decision, thus, art is a private and advertising a public matter.

Advertising, though detached from time and space, requires a
different kind of time than an artwork. Since advertising knows it
is force-fed to its target group (and many unintended bystanders)
and has little time to convey an image or a message, the piece of
information must be stripped of all unnecessary meanings which
would invite for contemplation. Even though advertising hopes to
establish a long-term relationship with the recipient, it knows well
that he or she will very soon be addressed by a different advertisement. The time available for conveying a message is thus that of
real-time, of the continuous, or as McLuhan remarks on TV commercials: "There simply is no time for the narrative form [...]"[52] A
work of art on the other hand invites contemplation and requires
a conscious effort to create one's understanding of it. A consumer
of a piece of art, when moved by it, perceives in a discontinuous
way, in a nonlinear, utopian (no-place) time, very much like the
time that elapses when engaging in intimate physical contact with
a living being.

---

50   Benjamin, The Work of Art in the Age of Mechanical Reproduction, 239.
        Similarly, McLuhan writes that "[a]ds are not meant for conscious con-
        sumption." McLuhan, Understanding Media, 228.
51   Buber, I and Thou, 65f. See also 60.
52   McLuhan, The Medium is the Massage, 126.

1.3   Communication as information transmission

If advertising is a vendor's cry it is addressed to a multitude of receivers but strangely enough, most of it forecloses the idea of crying back. An example of the impotence of one-way information is given to us by Astrid Lindgren, the great author of children's books:

> The children passed a perfume shop. In the window sat a big can of freckle salve. Next to the can was a cardboard sign which read: "Do you suffer from freckles?" [...]
> "Yes, surely", Pippi said thoughtfully, "a polite question demands a polite answer. Come on, we shall go inside."
> She opened the door and entered [...] Behind the counter was an elderly lady. Pippi went right up to her.
> "No", she said forcefully.
> "What would you like?" the lady asked.
> "No", Pippi repeated.
> "I don't understand what you mean", the lady said.
> "No, I do not suffer from freckles", Pippi said. Now the lady understood. She glanced at Pippi and exclaimed:
> "Yes, but dear child, your entire face is filled with freckles!"
> "Yes, certainly", Pippi said, "but I don't suffer from them. I like them. Good morning!"[53]

The cardboard sign in the perfume shop of Pippi's town is not designed for an answer. Pippi, although acting in an unexpected way, knows that if she wants to answer the question of the sign, she has to take recourse to the lady who owns the shop. The situation turns doubly comical because Pippi refuses to contextualise her "No." and because she takes the sign's question literally. The

---

53   Lindgren, Pippi Langstrumpf, 144.

sign is there to convey something but never—even if it displays a question—to engage in contact. It implicitly and technically closes itself off to any living subject. The advertising sign is always the foreigner and never the host.

If we briefly consider computer technology, we might understand at a technical level the obsession with one-way technologies: symmetrical communication blocks the system until the answer arrives while asymmetrical communication allows the computer to continue calculating, to remain conscious. If the lady at the perfume shop had to engage in symmetrical advertising, if she had to stand in front of her store and ask passers-by whether they suffered from freckles, she would not be able to work inside the store at the same time.

The overdetermination we observed on the level of response (buy/not buy) and the functional exchangeability of consumers in the eyes of commercial communications point to an understanding of communication as mere one-way information transmission. The overdetermination on the level of the creation of the message, that is, the involvement of multiple points of view signing as one entity, eradicate the possibility of a single speaker to take recourse to. A similar confusion happens at the level of who is spoken to. Commercial communications address an amorphous target, most frequently "the masses" or a segment thereof. Advertising cannot address a singularity because it cannot know who it speaks to—just like that singularity cannot know who is speaking.[54]

It appears as if this understanding of communication as information transmission is deliberately chosen. The classical advertising media are one-way media: newspaper ads, TV and radio commercials, billboards and, to a lesser degree, direct mailings

---

54   This might of course be different with personal recommendations, which is why new forms of advertising such as viral marketing enjoy a growing popularity in the industry.

and web banners. They only allow for a binary code of action, act/ not act, which frequently takes place where the advertisement is not, and do not incorporate any other type of feedback, such as "please leave me alone" or "I love your ad". The advertising complex is well aware of this aporia but instead of designing ways that allow for feedback, or feed-forward-back, it invests at the level of the creation of the message by buying "high-quality" addresses, carefully choosing the advertising media the target group is expected to see and conducting pre- and post-tests. In other words: instead of learning who will not want to see a particular message, it targets a segment of "the masses" in such a way that the advertising agency's client is convinced that the reasons for the chosen segment are based on profound knowledge of certain key factors attributed to the segment.

The present disregard of two-way-channel advertising cannot only be explained by the traditional, habitual practice of one-way communication, the know-how in measuring success and the long-standing experience of dealing with the binary response. It can also be attributed to a lack of technical proficiency and the fear that no one might reply. A quick look at some websites specifically designed for advertising indicates that this fear might be real.

To come back to Virilio's observation about Berlusconi quoted above:[55] if no one speaks and no one is spoken to, then no one can perceive no one's answer. The feedback mechanisms initiated at the level of the creation of the message, which eventually lead to its overdetermination, come to a halt precisely where they should have their starting point. When the World Federation of Advertisers stresses the role of the consumer ("We must reach our consumers on their terms, when they decide and through the means they choose."[56]; "Marketers need to better understand multi-media

55   Virilio, Ereignislandschaft, 32.
56   World Federation of Advertisers 2005 Annual Report, 2.

behaviour in order to reach their target consumer in a timely and respectful manner and at a receptive moment."[57]) it indicates that it is with the consumer and not the board of creation that a dialectic relationship must be sought in the first place. As a consequence of this failure to include the recipient in the process, we witness an enormous squandering of information. This squandering serves as a double self-defense mechanism. It allows for a noncommittal attitude at the ends of both the sender and the receiver: advertising can be functionally replaced by other advertising and potential buyers can be replaced by other potential buyers.

One might ask whether it is desirable that it should be possible to answer to a piece of advertising in the first place. When Maurice Blanchot talks about literature, he observes how the work of literature vanishes for the author the moment he makes it public. It becomes the work of someone else, the work "in which they are and he is not."[58] He goes on to say that "the author who writes for an audience in reality does not write: it is the audience who writes, and for this reason, it can no longer be the reader."[59] If the author (or a number of authors) of an advertisement writes for an audience, hence does not write, if the piece he or she puts in the world is no longer in his or her hands because it is being written by the audience, why should this audience be able to take recourse to the author? The difference lies in the overdetermination, in the kitsch, we could say. The advertisement as such is overdetermined in that it asks those who are receptive to it to act upon it in a way that exceeds the mere (literal) reading of the advertisement—without the author being present. It requires that the reader make a connection between the advertisement and his or her life and transform it into a material act *only in relation to the advertiser (author)* but

---

57   Ibid., 20.
58   Blanchot, Die Literatur und das Recht auf den Tod, 25.
59   Ibid., 27.

it does not provide the infrastructure to do it where the advertisement is read (respectively written).

1.4   The disappearance of critical distance

Part of the overabundance of messages can be attributed to the technical reproducibility without which there simply would not be enough manpower to spread messages in large numbers across our lives. The exchangeability of consumers and the exchangeability of advertising messages seem to legitimise the vast number of unseen, unheard, unfelt messages. If no one cares, there might as well be one more billboard, spam mail, advertisement.

Can we under these circumstances talk of a disappearance of critical distance? Is it not that the overabundance of messages goes hand-in-hand with an automatic reappropriation of distance due to a lack of involvement? Who must become distant to what or whom and with what goal? Does non-reaction affirm the existing power relationships, as Slavoj Žižek claims?[60] The linear structure of this book requires that these questions remain on hold for another while and that we will for the time being work with the hypothesis that we are faced with a certain disappearance of critical distance.

When advertising continuously occupies more public and private spaces, when ski resorts and mountain villages (where Nietzsche would have withdrawn to) are equipped with billboards and the teletopoi that connect us in real-time to distant people are infiltrated by telemarketers, when the wave of bad news in the newspaper is only balanced by the good news on the advertising pages,[61] it becomes difficult to withdraw. When the hand that feeds

60   Žižek, Die Revolution steht bevor, 45.
61   Lapham, in McLuhan, Understanding Media: "McLuhan notices correctly,

us is also feeding us advertising, it becomes nearly impossible to take distance.

When we look at the term "critical distance", we need to ask what critique is in the first place. Michel Foucault answers: "the art of not being governed or better, the art of not being governed like that and at that cost."[62] Nietzsche suggests in the figure of Zarathustra the importance of contemplative withdrawal to gather strength which enables him to come down from the mountain and bear witness to what he has learned far away from the market vendors' cries.[63] This withdrawal is also what "distance" implies: the standing apart from each other.[64] In the excerpts quoted, we can see a difference in the attitude between Nietzsche and Pippi Longstocking. Nietzsche's discontent with the hustle and bustle of civilisation requires a conscious effort to find quietude,[65] while Pippi plunges headlong into that civilisation to answer unasked questions. Nietzsche is so immersed that he needs to withdraw while Pippi is so withdrawn that she can easily immerse. Her natural light-heartedness is the actual "art of not being governed" that Zarathustra preaches, but—in the gravity of his speech—cannot quite convince us that he has already internalised.[66] Even though Nietzsche "makes joyousness a new prerequisite of scientific endeavour"[67] it is not something which comes naturally to him. He is only the prophet of the philosophers to come, he is not the philosopher of the future himself. While Pippi is a girl naturally gifted

that it is the bad news [...] that sells the good news—that is, the advertisements" (xvi). It also works the other way round: the good news (advertising) in fact sell the bad news (the news of the world) by paying a considerable share for the latter's dissemination.

62   Foucault, The Essential Foucault, 265.
63   Nietzsche, Also sprach Zarathustra.
64   KLUGE, "Distanz", 205.
65   Nietzsche, Gay Science, §331.
66   In "Pippi og Sokrates" Gaare and Sjaastad discuss at length parallels between Astrid Lindgren's characters and leading Western philosophers.
67   Ronell, The Test Drive, 154.

with dance, Zarathustra is still learning his steps. Pippi has a plastic, creative ease of handling civilisation, if we accept Gossage's notion that creativity may come from a deficiency of seeing things "in a normal fashion."[68]

Let us attempt to substantiate why there should be a general disappearance of the distance required not to be governed to such an extent. Virilio's oeuvre reminds us that a shift is taking place, a shift in which he sees a disappearance of distances. "Real", electronic time at the speed of light (the synthesis of time and distance which reduces distance to an imperceptible length), i.e. a quantitative, physical time, is replacing intensive, qualitative time. Communications accelerate, take off into orbit and instantaneity becomes the leading paradigm of information, replacing "audio-visual proximity and relatively confined intervals or territories" which characterise "natural" communications[69] and depriving us of the time needed to reflect.[70] "A message that takes itself seriously always needs a certain time for reflection [...]"[71] Virilio would call this mental pollution but it might be more precise to say that this inaugurates a process of mental disinfection. Growing up in an environment dominated by real, quantitative time, our immune system becomes used to it and consequently grows stronger—a mental flexibility which keeps us from getting infected too easily but at the same time robs us of our ability to shape our environment. This flexibility is biologically given by our brain's ability to

---

68   Gossage, The Book of Gossage, 38.
69   Virilio, Eroberung des Körpers, 16.
70   An anecdote: Travelling back by train to Zurich from a seminar with Virilio in France, immersed in a book of Virilio's, the ticket collector proudly announced on 4 Apr 2007 at around 1.45pm, half an hour after it had taken place, that the SNCF had set a new speed record of 574,8 kmh. Arriving at Zurich 2½ h later, the newspaper "Heute" with this piece of news was already being distributed. This is fast, no doubt, but let us remember that Edison, when he was young, sold newspapers he produced on the train.
71   Virilio, Krieg und Fernsehen, 63.

physically adjust to our environment in a process of a plasticity of modification, but this is only half the story since plasticity also means the ability to form and not only to be formed.

We should leave this ambiguity, this pollution or hyperinfection of cause and effect in suspension and remember that Derrida claims "there is no time to take time, a number of well-meaning contemporaries will undoubtedly say—as if the events had not always precipitated themselves."[72] Not only is the time span it takes for an event to happen generally shorter than the time its reflection requires, which can be attributed to the chemical reactions required to make synaptic connections. Speed and the command over a future course of events triggered by an information advantage has always been a matter of proportion, of being faster than the others: from Marathon to Napoleon's telegraph and the Gulf Wars' real-time media coverage.

Perhaps we should try to trace the disappearance of critical distance elsewhere, in a realm more occupied with mental space than with physical space. Advertising addresses physical bodies which are divided into private and public functions and—this is not the same—into consumers and citizens.[73] It addresses the consumer in the citizen's environment claiming a right to "freedom of expression" just as much as it addresses the private person in his or her private environment. The International Advertising Association in its mission statement sees itself as "an advocate for freedom of choice for individuals across all *consumer and business markets*"[74] while elsewhere it is "committed to the principle of free choice for all *citizens.*"[75] Peter Leutenegger, then vice-president of "Schweizer

---

72   Derrida, Politik der Freundschaft, 117. I was unable to trace this passage in the English translation *The Politics of Friendship.*

73   Hänggi, Out-of-home advertising in the twenty-first century: the sell-out of public space? 79.

74   IAA Global, "Our Mission". http://www.iaaglobal.org (16 Oct 2008).

75   Ibid., "Programs – Advertising and Constitutional Protection". The passage

Werbung SW" and CEO of the advertising agency FCB Leutenegger Krüll (now DraftFCB/Lowe-Group) is quoted in an SW brochure: "With great commitment, Schweizer Werbung SW fights at the forefront against advertising bans and thus for the rights of the *citizen* to free information."[76] Derrida observes that "[t]he individualism of technological civilisation relies precisely on a misunderstanding of the unique self. It is an individualism relating to a *role* and not a *person.*"[77] The advertising industry has difficulties grappling with the concept of a unique self, a person who cannot be replaced by another person; consequently it designates a number of roles to assign to the target persons—consumer, listener, viewer, generation x, DINK (double income no kids). This drive for categories for better understanding certain social strata to be targeted at once has led to some unfortunate categories such as the citizen, which, as a concept is nothing to be treated by the domain of commercial communications but politics, and some confusions of categories, such as that of the consumer and the citizen.

When "private" signifies the family domain and "public" the political domain,[78] it is not at all clear where a potential economic domain could legitimately enter. A confusion of a similar sort already roots in the Greek agora, which designated a gathering as well as the marketplace and its commodities—thus the exercise of rights at specific locations on public grounds. In an address to the conference of the European ministers of education, Adolf Muschg explained the functions of the agora: "[On the agora], people bargained over the price of goods, like on any market in the

quoted is no longer accessible via the Website of IAA Global but it can be found through search engines and the Wayback Machine on the Internet Archive http://www.archive.org. (12 Apr 2007). Italics mine.

76   Schweizer Werbung, Ein Portrait, 8 (italics mine). The "great commitment" is not that great, as Karl Lüönd complains in an article in Werbewoche. Lüönd, "Bis zur Bewusstlosigkeit?".

77   Derrida, The Gift of Death, 36.

78   Dictionary of Sociology, "Public sphere versus private sphere distinction".

world; and at the same time, like on no other market in the world, they argued over the value and the order of things."[79] These two spheres however did not entirely pervade each other: "On the classical agora, the city square [Ratplatz] and the market were tightly linked and simultaneously divided by an invisible line: it divided the sphere of commerce and exchange from that of political decision-making."[80] Thus, "public sphere" refers not only to physical public grounds but also to "the open discussion among members of a collectivity about their common concerns", thus to a mental environment.[81] "Public" according to Hannah Arendt signifies on the one hand everything that appears before the general public ("Allgemeinheit"), for everyone to see and hear, and, on the other hand, the world itself as that which we share and which is distinct from what is private.[82] All these significations of public and public sphere may be synthesised in the assumption that what shapes everybody's mental environment is likely to shape everybody's sensory environment—and vice versa.

It is here that we should locate a disappearance of critical distance, in these entangled notions of the public and the private, the consumer and the citizen, family, politics and economy because this allows us to diagnose a lack of critical distance on both the side of the sender (foreigner) and the receiver (host). If we accept the three domains of the private, the political and the economical as cornerstones of our civilisation (the religious proposed as belonging to the private), which each have functions within their respective domain and functions reaching out to the other two, these relationships have to be disentangled to understand their nature and delimit their claims on the other domains. We cannot fail to observe a fusion, a confusion of these domains. On the level of

79   Muschg, Schule Europa, B1.
80   Ibid.
81   Dictionary of the Social Sciences, "Public sphere".
82   Arendt, Vita activa, 62–65.

public-economic con/fusion we see public-private partnerships, the mall as public sphere, the inroads of consumer brands into schools, but also issues of authorship and copyright.[83] While the agora was the place for marketing goods and for public discussion, the former has spread out over the entire city and the latter has retreated into parliament and municipal buildings and the private home. On the level of the dissolution of the economic and the private, we can refer to the inroads of advertising into our private lives by means of our teletopoi.[84] And finally, the private and the political domains fall together in the control of certain communication channels by national (state or private) entities and the legal framework, which should guarantee the maximum amount of liberty to the maximum number of people.[85]

There is a growing number of delimited physical spaces where all three domains come together. Most often they are conceptualised as shopping centres, incorporating also public squares, housing—and sometimes a chapel.[86] It is indicative of the domination of the economic domain over the public and private domains, that the shopping or passive consumption aspect in these projects is usually stressed over the other aspects.

---

83   For public-private partnerships see Klein, *No Logo*. For authorship and copyright issues, see: Lessig, *Free Culture*.
84   See Virilio's *Open Sky*, among others, and Derrida's *Of Hospitality*, 49ff.
85   Two random examples may further illustrate this overlap of the public and the private domain: (1) The Swiss Federal Council has decided that it is legal for political parties to deposit unsolicited mail before elections and popular votes in letterboxes with a sticker refusing advertising. (2) In the USA, the practice of anal sex, even between consenting adults, is prohibited in a number of states.
86   Sihlcity, a multi-purpose complex opened 2007 in Zurich. The HTML description meta tag reads: "Sihlcity—a new district in Zurich's south end. The diverse range of products and services on a total area of more that 100 000sqm includes several restaurants, movie theatres, a disco, a cultural spot, a health and wellness centre, a hotel, a shopping mall as well as areas reserved for services and condominiums." http://www.sihlcity.ch. (16 Oct 2008).

In his novel *The Cave*, José Saramago tells the story of a family who is economically forced to move into The Center, a gigantic complex of shops and apartments (not "apartments and shops") which should take care of all their needs. The ground beneath is continuously carved out to create more space within the confines of the Center, until the construction workers discover something which terrifies them: Plato's cave. At this moment, the family can see where they are headed and decide to leave the Center:

> After a few kilometres, Marçal said [...], There was a poster, one of those really big ones outside the Center, can you guess what it said, he asked. We've no idea, they replied, and, as if he were reciting something, Marçal said COMING SOON, PUBLIC OPENING OF PLATO'S CAVE, AN EXCLUSIVE ATTRACTION, UNIQUE IN THE WORLD, BUY YOUR TICKET NOW.[87]

1.5   The price of communication

By your ticket now. The entangled domains of the private, the political and the economic are in many ways dominated by the economic under the precept of a free market economy: "The economic laws penetrate all areas of life, so that we take them for granted like the laws of gravity", Al Gore remarks.[88] Money, the currency of conversion provided by the economy, allows for the comparing of material and non-material things to take place, something soft factors or moral values often fail to accomplish, supposing that supply and demand will take care of the right monetary value. In advertising, this currency enters a circle of auto-efficiency or auto-logic, as advertising man Howard Gossage testifies:

---

87   Saramago, The Cave, 307.
88   Gore, Wege zum Gleichgewicht, 181.

But since ours is a competitive business in an open economic system, our services are for sale to the highest bidder; and the highest
bidders are just those who have the highest profit margins—usually
because they have little intrinsic worth—most of their value is con-
tributed by the advertising they buy so freely.[89]

This self-promoting circle is further aggravated by a kind of logic
which sees the role of advertising embedded in and as a guaran-
tor for a free market economy or for free speech. This distinction
must be deconstructed. On the one hand, free market economy is
not free, and on the other hand, free market economy has a narrow temporal and spatial field of vision which leads to goods and
services not being given a price tag which reflects their sustainable use. The ecobalance, or lifecycle assessment, is nothing but
the conversion of chemical, biological and physical facts to a set of
binary values (ecologically friendy/ecologically damaging), which
is then modelled on another set of binary values in another system
such as the economic (money/no money; have/not have), the legal
(legal/illegal) or the sciencific (true/not true).[90]

The question whether the ecobalance should incorporate these
assets or loss thereof and give the products a perhaps equally arbitrary monetary value is to remain ambivalent. While the consumers will not become aware of the actual damage their purchases
cause for generations to follow, there is always a certain danger
that such an inclusion of non-material values in the monetary
economy could cause a neutralisation. A price tag alone, as high
as it might be, would in fact be a mere trade-off against the bad
conscience caused by the shamelessness of the price tag.[91]

---

89   Gossage, Is There Any Hope for Advertising? 5.
90   Siegenthaler, Ökobilanz, 14–16.
91   See: Braungart and McDonough, Einfach intelligent produzieren, 86.

The belief that free market economy is free is a misconception of the word "free", just like freedom of speech is not free. It is not free in two senses. Firstly, it is constrained by the political domain, the economic domain, by moral restrictions and by restrictions due to deficiencies in leading theories of political economy—restrictions both on the levels of positive and negative freedom. In political systems which guarantee freedom of speech, we are allowed to say what we want—but not necessarily where, when and to whom we want. Secondly, and most obviously, neither the free market nor free speech (with the exception of speaking to a person nearby) is *gratis*, free of cost.

A parenthesis on the etymology of "free", which contrasts the idea of a free market and takes us to the issue of sustainability: Martin Heidegger reports that "[t]he word for peace, *Friede*, means the free, das *Frye*; and *fry* means preserved from harm and danger, preserved from something, safeguarded. To free actually means to spare."[92] Thus, the idea of freedom of communication is not only thought to be a guardian of peace, it also means that this peace can only be guaranteed—can only be sustainable—when guided by care, by preserving and sparing.

Legal restrictions on advertising are increasingly discussed and implemented. These concern products or attitudes considered harmful to all or specific audiences, such as tobacco, alcohol or sex. One of the more prominent arguments the advertising industry brings forth is that it should be legal to advertise for products that are legal.[93] In many discussions with advertising practitioners, issues of the legality of their work come up in a way that not only eclipses the question of legitimacy but also condemns acts of discontent (such as adbusting[94]) as illegal and violating property.

---

92   Heidegger, Basic Writings, 351.
93   Allianz gegen Werbeverbote (Alliance against advertising bans).
94   On adbusting, see: Klein, No Logo, 279–446.

While the advertisers hide behind the issue of legality and do not see what might be wrong as long as they comply with the (somewhat arbitrary) local laws, every campaign that carries some legal risk (showing skin, depicting hard liquor in a certain manner, guerrilla marketing on public grounds, etc.) already has a budget included to pay the fines that may arise. The weight of this budget depends on the legal system where a campaign is run. Many legal texts do not make a difference between a violation of the law by a private person (i.e. an announcement of a yard sale) and by a corporation. What could break a private person's neck is simply another budgetary item for corporations. Consequently, fines buy "free" speech. They are a remission, an *Ablass*, and do not explicitly serve to deter from breaking the law, be it legitimate or not.

The narrow field of vision of the free market economy has led to an attitude which calculates only a share of the effective costs and benefits. Progress is measured in GDP or other indicators, which eclipses costs that do not enter the annual balance sheet and costs which have to be carried by others. Some of these costs, environmental costs for instance, will even rise with negative growth factors: the product causing pollution goes into one balance sheet and the costs of removing the waste go into another balance sheet, so that a nation which has a lot of environmental damages to get rid of, will actually have a higher GDP—a higher measurable indicator for progress.[95, 96] The economic system as it is applied today fails to calculate resources such as clean water and air, but also non-physical goods such as the distress of the mental or visual environment. Again, calculating these in monetary terms is ambivalent and might result in a trade-off of value and price. In

---

95   Gore, Wege zum Gleichgewicht, 187.
96   The *Exxon Valdez* accident in 1989 led to a higher GDP in Alaska. The reason was that many more people were present in the state to remove environmental damages (Braungart and McDonough, Einfach intelligent produzieren, 57).

Wolfgang Schirmacher's words: "We need to know the true price of everything, not only the arbitrarily determined because there is only one balance sheet; it is the only world that is perishing."[97] When he speaks of the "true price" it is not to be misunderstood as the true monetary equivalent but as the "true praise", the "true appraisal".

CPM (or CPT), cost per thousand contacts, is a frequently used currency of conversion between advertising spaces in different media. The term "cost" is somewhat misleading. CPM is the *price* someone pays to the owner of the medium for an advertisement, not the *costs* involved. The larger the audience, generally said, the lower the price per unit: in 2005, cinema was the most expensive advertising medium at a CPM of $59.43, while outdoor advertising was the cheapest at an average of $5.37.[98] CPM usually reflects the expected exposure, but fails to put a number to the spectator's involvement or, more importantly, non-involvement. If only 3% of the population is able to recall unaided a billboard advertisement, the cost of all those whose field of vision the billboard trespasses without leaving noticeable mental traces must be internalised because the growth of advertising messages inevitably leads to a decline in the recall rate: "The very bulk of advertising is its worst enemy because somewhere along the line an immunity starts building up against irritation."[99] The low CPM does not make the billboard a more democratic advertising medium since those with large advertising budgets just buy all the more. It does not come as a surprise that outdoor advertising still enjoys a growing popularity among advertisers when they only pay half a cent to trespass someone's field of vision.

---

97   Schirmacher, Ereignis Technik, 46.
98   World Federation of Advertisers 2005 Annual Report, 23.
99   Gossage, Is There Any Hope for Advertising? 7.

There is also another peculiarity in the accounting mechanisms of the advertising industry which Gossage points to: the commission system, which is rather a kickback system. The agency is given a kickback, usually between 10 and 15%, for advertising space they buy. This means that the more money the advertising agency spends in the name of its client, the more it earns.[100] The more that is squandered, the higher the riches are. This is a beautiful example of an economy of excess, which will be discussed in further detail in the next chapter. This economy of excess is a positive growth factor as long as it does not lead to a careless use of its own resources.

1.6 Conclusion

We touched a number of topics that can be considered exemplary of the advertising complex's failure to project a sustainable and productive development in the field of communication; a sustainable development which would not only solve the challenges the advertising complex faces today but most of all—and this is not contradictory—liberate the mind of the consumer/citizen to such an extent that he or she is able to achieve a higher mental productivity. To summarise, we criticised, under the umbrella of an instrumental view of communication, the blurred distinction between natural persons and legal persons; the idea of communication as one-way information transmission; the loss of critical distance; and the attribution of monetary values to communication acts.

After all these considerations, risking to state a commonplace notion which can be observed in many discussions with people working in the advertising complex, we might say that the

---

100 Ibid., 9.

advertising complex is not able to let go of these contradictory no-tions and practices because it is the way one, they, *man* (German), *on* (French), does it and has done it for considerable time. There simply is no other perspective when one is immersed in working in that field. The responsibility is shared, that is, dissolved in the organisational complex.

To conclude this chapter, it seems fitting to let Heidegger char-acterise the "They", the *Man*, an idea or a term or a concept which is closely linked to the public and in everyday use is responsible for levelling out differences between singularities and adjusting to an imposed flexibility.

> The *Man* is present everywhere, but in a way that it has already always sneaked away where Dasein pushes for a decision. Because the *Man* provides all judgment and decision, it takes the responsibility off the respective Dasein. The *Man* can quasi afford that "*man*" always takes recourse to it. It can most easily be responsible for everything be-cause there is no one who needs to account for something.[101]

---

101   Heidegger, Sein und Zeit, 127

2 Communication as being-with-others

2.1 Etymological considerations

Communication has become a ruling term of the self-conception not only of human communication but also of information transfer in the economic sector. This has become a somewhat problematic undertaking as there are too many kinds of "communications" around that each follow their own rules. The following definitions exemplify the conflicts we are faced with when we try to understand what communication means:

Communication: 1. Understanding between each other, commerce, traffic. 2. Connection, interrelation.[102]

Borrowed from Latin communicatio (-onis) "Message", abstract of Latin communicare "convey, share, divide, make common", to Latin communis "collective, common, together".[103]

---

102 Duden Fremdwörterbuch, 5. Auflage. Original: "Kommunikation: 1. Verständigung untereinander, Umgang, Verkehr. 2. Verbindung, Zusammenhang."
103 KLUGE. Original: "Kommunikation: Entlehnt aus l. communication (-onis) 'Mitteilung', Abstraktum von l. communicare 'mitteilen, teilen, gemeinschaftlich machen', zu l. communis 'gemeinschaftlich, allgemein, gemeinsam."

Communication: (from Latin communicare, make common, partake (let partake), discuss), transfer of messages.[104]

The basic conflict is that of whether communication is one-way or several-ways. The significations of the term "communication" we quoted may be divided into two understandings, one of which seems to be included in the other. One (message transfer) implies an asymmetric relationship, a one-way transfer, an imbalance of sorts; the other (making common) implies a technically symmetric relationship between the communicants, a several-way transfer, a feed-forward-back, a balance over time. When we set up a mirror before the asymmetric message transfer to obtain a kind of feedback, a knowledge which is "shared (divided) by both and yet autonomous on both sides of the glass of the mirror",[105] we are already in the reciprocity of making common.

When *communicatio* is translated into German *Mitteilung*, message, to what is shared with, or divided with, it at first implies an asymmetric relationship between who shares (divides) and who is shared (divided) with: someone gives something to someone else. Sharing-with can be two-fold. When we share goods, we divide them, give away a part and keep the rest. When we share thoughts, we give them away entirely and keep them in their entirety; when a thought is given away, it is multiplied and not transferred. The word *Mit-teilung* implies a gift, a partial *(Teil)* gift which at the same time is not at all partial: it does not exhaust itself since it is still there when given away. It is no longer secreted, disclosed, kept in the dark, but made common.[106]

---

104   Hügli/Lübcke, Philosophielexikon. Original: "Kommunikation: (von lat. communicare, gemeinsam machen, teilnehmen lassen, sich besprechen), Übertragung von Mitteilungen."
105   Derrida, The Politics of Friendship, 194f.
106   When a secret is shared it is the sharing-with which discloses and multiplies the message but annuls the character of a secret. For further ruminations on

Why this emphasis on the non-exhaustive character and the question of "*free*dom of speech" in the last chapter? In economic theory the two characteristics of a public good are its non-rivalry ("one person's consumption does not detract from or prevent another person's consumption") and its non-excludability (it is not "possible to exclude any individual from the benefits of the public good").[107] Public goods should last for generations and have thus a quality of sustainability. Presently, there is little awareness in political practice and in urban and media planning that the mental environment is also a public good or a common-property resource, as Lasn notes.[108]

2.2   The gift of communication

"Communication as transfer" and "communication as making common" can be linked to the gift. The gift, according to Derrida, would be related to economy but at the same time be that which interrupts economy, that which "no longer gives rise to an exchange."[109] Its conditions are forgetfulness, non-appearance, non-phenomenality, non-perception and non-keeping.[110] In this he takes a different viewpoint than Marcel Mauss who claims that a gift always requires a countergift.[111] For this to happen it must be apparent, perceived and remembered. In the conclusion of his inquiry into gift-giving and potlatch traditions of ancient and indigenous peoples, Mauss adapts some of his findings to the present

the secret, see Montaigne (Derrida/Montaigne, Über die Freundschaft, 82) and Derrida (The Gift of Death, 82ff).

107   Stiglitz, Economics of the Public Sector, 128.
108   Lasn, Culture Jam, 13.
109   Derrida, Given Time, 7.
110   Ibid., 15.
111   Mauss, The Gift.

westernised cultures. He recognises the asymmetric character of the gift, but at the same time makes the shift we proposed above, to set a mirror up to the initial act of giving (or of communicating) and in this way give the doubled act a notion of symmetry. Mauss observes that we still think that "to give is to show one's superiority […] To accept without giving in return, or without giving more back, is to become client and servant, to fall lower."[112] The gift enters an economic cycle, a spiral spinning faster with every turn: what is given back must at least be of equal value, if not higher.[113] Derrida's gift, on the other hand, is *the* impossible, that which must not be exhausted by the process of exchange, that which must not circulate.[114] It is fundamentally asymmetric but in a strangely symmetric way: neither the donor nor the donee must be aware of the gift for "*the intentional meaning of the gift*, in order for this simple recognition of the gift as gift" (italics mine) would immediately annul it.[115] The recognition of the gift would make it part of the asymmetric circulation Mauss attributes to gift-giving.

A note on asymmetry and dissymmetry: The German translation of Derrida's *Politics of Friendship* uses the word *Asymmetrie* while the English translation and the French original use *dissymmetry*. Symmetry refers to *symmetria, sýmmetros*: measured,

---

112   Mauss, The Gift, 74.
113   This lies also at the core of most privately funded sponsoring activities of cultural or public goods. No corporation would sponsor something if this were not allowed to become public, which contrasts the Biblical command in Matthew 6: 1–4 Derrida invokes towards the end of *The Gift of Death*: "Therefore when thou doest thine alms, do not sound a trumpet before thee, as the hypocrites do in the synagogues and in the streets, that they may have glory of men. […] That thine alms may be in secret; and thy Father which seeth in secret himself shall reward thee openly." (Derrida, The Gift of Death, 108). Even so, when one does not have the glory of men, one is rewarded later.
114   Derrida, Given Time, 7, 12.
115   Ibid., 14.

proportionate, harmonious.[116] A quick glance through a number of dictionaries[117] revealed that both words should exist in French, English and German even though in some dictionaries only one or the other appears, usually asymmetry. None of the dictionaries give sufficient reason to use one and not the other. The Micro-Robert defines *asymétrie* as absence of symmetry and *dissymétrie* as a defect (*défaut*) of symmetry; the Duden Fremdwörterbuch, conversely, defines *Asymmetrie* as a defect (*Mangel*) of symmetry or as *Ungleichmässigkeit*, inequality, imbalance. According to KLUGE, the prefix *a-* refers to the opposite or a lack of a certain quality and the prefix *dis-* refers to a negation. We shall opt for a use of "asymmetry" because it conveys more of a sense of a state of imbalance and not so much a movement towards imbalance; asymmetry implies a certain hope in a struggle for balance while dissymmetry reads more resigned.

2.2.1 Question and answer

In many languages, one *gives* an answer *(Antwort geben; donner une réponse)*. The German "das Du *geben*" (French: *tutoyer*; to be on first-name terms), to give the You to someone, is a gift which is most often practiced as a reciprocal gift *("sich das Du geben"; "se tutoyer"),* the gift which is at the basis of an intimate relationship, of a relationship which enables the "I" in the first place.[118] We can give and receive this You, this Thou.[119] This is also inherent in "asking a question". What may appear as a tautology: *eine Frage fragen*[120] becomes the request for reciprocity, a request for the gift of another question.

116 KLUGE, "Symmetrie".
117 Duden Fremdwörterbuch; KLUGE; Oxford Advanced Learner's Dictionary; Le Micro-Robert; LEO.
118 Buber, I and Thou, 37.
119 Ibid., 12.
120 "Eine Frage stellen", to pose a question, is the usual German wording.

Referring back to Pippi Longstocking's story, we can apply this question of reciprocity to find the difference between two situations: 1) The cardboard sign asking Pippi "Do you suffer from freckles?" and 2) Pippi's friend Annika asking her "Do you suffer from freckles?" The first situation is in fact not all that different from a freckle salve salesperson asking her "Do you suffer from freckles?" It requires that Pippi *give an answer, even though it really already contains the answer.* The real answer that is aimed at is the purchase of the product. The second situation requires that Pippi *give another question* (such as: "No, why do you think I would?"), an undetermined question (answer) which, either way it is asked (answered), would be the opening of a common future. For this counter-question to take place there need not be a question mark at the end of the sentence; any utterance will do if it marks the beginning of a common future. This reciprocity of asking a question is elucidated, in a commonplace way perhaps, in that who gives is who receives.[121] When there is only reception or only giving, we cannot speak of communication as we cannot speak of community.

The saleswoman or the cardboard sign require an answer and the only one they are interested in is affirmative. Hence, the only permissible counter-question is something along the lines of "Yes, why do you ask?" Unless one of the participants breaks the unwritten laws of intended behaviour, the answer or the counter-question marks the beginning of an end of the relationship. The cardboard sign's unwritten answer "Buy this freckle salve!" is already prepared, already determined within the initial question.

What about answering an answer? Is this the same as asking a question? Derrida seems to privilege thinking in answers and speaks of the virtual answer to the answer: "Invited to speak to you, while you would be alone or assembled to listen to me, then

---

to examine me—in short: to answer me—I have already answered an invitation and am therefore addressing you who are beginning to answer me."[122] This answer is still virtual concerning the contents but it is already real in the attention paid to the speaker,[123] just like attending (in the sense of waiting) has the virtual object of whom or what one is waiting for, but whose object is already real in that it is what one is waiting for.

To answer means to respond to *(antworten, répondre à)*, but also to answer for, to be responsible for *(verantwortlich sein, répondre de)* and to answer before *(sich verantworten, répondre devant)*. Derrida again:

> These three modalitites are not juxtaposable; they are enveloped and implied in one another. One *answers for*, for self or for something (for someone, for an action, a thought, a discourse), *before* an other, a community of others, an institution, a court, a law. And always one *answers for* (for self or for its intention, its action or discourse), *before*, by first responding *to*: this last modality thus appearing more originary, more fundamental and hence unconditional.[124]

This sketch of interdependences of the different meanings and interpretations of answer will suffice for the moment.

If we had replaced *asking* a question with *posing* a question, the matters would not change entirely. Posing indicates that something is put before someone and it is up to the latter to grab it. It is like placing a big question mark before an interlocutor and the real question is not "what is the answer?" but "what do you do with this?"[125] When someone poses as someone or something,

122 Derrida, The Politics of Friendship, 229.
123 Ibid., 229.
124 Ibid., 250 (italics his).
125 I have not been able to pursue the reasons for which we do not say "eine Frage fragen" or "quest a question" (for *quaerere* means to ask, but also to

when someone strikes a pose, there occurs a transformation of the poser. He or she is no longer the same as before the act of posing—but still remains the same. Certain qualities of the poser change to assimilate those of who or what is posed as. If Christian posed as Pippi, he would perhaps braid his hair into two pigtails or put on shoes that are much too large. Nevertheless, he still remains the same person. The likeness occurs in the mind of those present at the moment of posing or of transformation. The moment we pose a question, it remains a question to be grabbed and transformed by the addressee, and this act of transformation gives it qualities of a virtual answer, an answer in both ways and a question in both ways.

2.2.2   Deferring the decision

Everything points to a *decision*, a decision which we should perhaps not yet make, which we are not ready to come to: a decision which is not ready to welcome us, but which we nevertheless must understand. Shall we consider communication as something which requires reciprocity, an economic cycle, a countergift; or is communication, like the gift and friendship, the gift of friendship, unilateral, asymmetric, non-cyclic? Is friendship fundamentally symmetric in that it calls for a fundamental asymmetry?

Decision, de-scission, *Ent-Scheidung* can be read as a tautology but also as an opposition which forces us to a conclusion.[126] The scission and the *Scheidung* already imply a divide, just as *mit-teilen* implies a divide; the de-scission might signal 1) a stress on this

---

seek, claim, acquire, probe) but I suspect it is primarily for reasons of linguistic taste and simplicity that we say "eine Frage stellen", "ask or pose a question".

126 Decision, scission etc. are also related to words such as schism and schizophrenia. *Schízein* is Greek for splitting (German: *spalten*) (KLUGE, "Schizophrenie").

division (a doubling of the scission), 2) a negation, an overcoming of the divide, or simply 3) a distancing *(ent-fernen)* of the person who is faced with the decision. First case: de-scission is that which not only makes us see that there is a scission: it is that which calls on us to reinforce that scission. It is that which forces us to give the scission a materiality, to decide in favour of either one or the other part. Second case: the second case might be linked to the third but we are tempted to lend it a different spatial metaphor. A negation of the scission asks us to take the materiality out of the scission, to unite the separate parts into one by vertically elevating ourselves above the problem so that we can overlook, overcome, the divide by seeing a larger picture. It is a decision that does not call for the either-or but the both-this-and-that, a decision which calls for the eternal perhaps. Third case: in the third case, we are once again faced with a decision. We can distance ourselves from the problem, or we can distance the problem from ourselves. Either way we horizontally take distance, thus we are not able to oversee the scission. We do not deny the problem altogether but we deny its applicability to our person. It is the decision which does not want to take place but which is nevertheless a decision and perhaps all the more a non-political political decision, keeping in mind what Ulrich Beck wrote on the younger generation's refusal to partici- pate in politics: the children of freedom [Kinder der Freiheit] "are an actively apolitical youth, because they suck the life out of the institutions which circle in themselves."[127] A highly political denial of politics,[128] and as such we might understand Derrida when he says that the "de-politicization is but the truth of the political."[129]

The impossibility of decision will come back to us at the thresh- old to the house and the question of the other who is allowed

---

127 Beck, Kinder der Freiheit, 14.
128 Ibid., 11.
129 Derrida, The Politics of Friendship, 247.

to trespass the threshold. This decision will also have a say in whether communication, or life, is being-with-others or rather being-for-others. Georges Bataille's considerations of the potlatch, which are rooted in Mauss' ideas of the gift,[130] cannot answer this question, but it is where we might find a moment of reconciliation between Derrida and Mauss. Bataille's concept of the accursed share is the energy surplus that all natural and cultural systems must expend in the back-and-forth of gift-giving in the broadest sense. He writes:

> [L]iving matter receives this [solar] energy and accumulates it within the limits given by the space that is available to it. It then radiates or squanders it, but before devoting an appreciable share to this radiation it makes maximum use of it for growth. [...] The limit of growth being reached, life, without being in a closed container, at least enters into ebullition: Without exploding, its extreme exuberance pours out in a movement always bordering on explosion.[131]

The giver of energy is the sun, a giver that gives a gift in Derrida's sense. It is unintentional and unknown to both the donor and the donee.[132] In the potlatch, where a chief offers his rival riches to humiliate, challenge and obligate him, the recipient, by accepting the gift, must later take up the challenge with a new potlatch exceeding the first in value.[133] This must continue until the system explodes. At the end of this to-and-fro is the ultimate gift, the impossible gift, the gift which for Bataille is death and which Derrida does not want to name. According to Bataille, death is besides sexuality

---

130 Luckow in Bataille, Das obszöne Werk, 226.
131 Bataille, The Accursed Share, 29–30.
132 Further down it will be shown that it does not exactly correspond to Derrida's idea of the gift and that the sun is not exactly the ideal model for this discussion.
133 Bataille, The Accursed Share, 67–69.

and eating (especially meat) the best example of a squandering of excess energy, a luxury of nature,[134] and much of Bataille's erotic work is devoted to bringing these three excesses together.[135] He recognises that, "[o]f all conceivable luxuries, death, in its fatal and inexorable form, is undoubtedly the most costly."[136] When death is given, there is no more reciprocity. The gift-giving relation is at a dead end. No one can surpass this gift because no one can give more than his or her life. Here, more than before, the German *Gift*, poison, resonates. Giving death is the impossible because the moment the gift is accepted and the life ended there is no giver anymore who gave and thus no giver to return a countergift to, a countergift which would top the unexceedable. This death is a double death: it ends the life of the giver and with it the life of the gift-giving relationship.

2.2.3   The gift of marriage

There is still another meaning of the gift that has been left unexplored. In Nordic languages, the word *gifte*, usually used as a reflexive (i.e. symmetric) verb such as the Norwegian *å gifte seg*,[137] does not refer to the gift (in Norwegian: *gave*. *Gift* in Norwegian, like in German, also means poison). Most significantly it translates to getting married. The marriage as a gift: the positive life-affirming way of giving yourself, of giving your life, of giving your life to someone, or rather: *to each other* "till death do you part". Here, "giving one's life" is not perverted into giving one's own death; it is taken literally to mean to dedicate the time one is given to someone else: to put one's life in someone else's hands without the violence of an asymmetric giving, or, more precisely: without the

---

134   Ibid., 33.
135   See for instance *The Story of the Eye* and *Blue of Noon*.
136   Bataille, *The Accursed Share*, 34.
137   Swedish: *gifta sig*; Danish: *gifte sig*.

violence of one-sided asymmetric giving. At the basis of this conception lies the perception of life as something which can be given away and kept at the same time. We are faced with a gift which is perhaps the closest we come to the gift which cannot be surpassed while still remaining in the realm of life, albeit with the horizon of the biological death. Yet this gift in many ways does not live up to Derrida's requirements of the ultimate, unspeakable, unknowable gift since, culturally, to marry someone is, or was until the notion of romantic love developed and beyond, closely related to a weighing of drawbacks and benefits, of status, of dowry or trousseau (German: *Mitgift*: that which is given with). It also does not live up to Derrida's requirements in that it is a performative act which can be annulled by the performative act of divorcing someone or divorcing from someone, which, even though this act may be performed on mutual understanding, in English and Norwegian lacks the linguistic mutuality, the symmetry of performance that is ambiguous in German: *sich scheiden lassen* (it is ambiguous in that *sich* may refer to oneself but also to each other). In that sense, to marry, *å gifte seg*, does not bear the finality of the strike of death and requires a certain cultural context in which it is performed, a context which further obfuscates any notions of a personal, private, intimate giving.

One could still argue that, without the cultural rituals and economic weighing of marriage that may be sidestepped by declaring one's love to each other, marriage is the kind of gift-giving which has the power to become an ethical paradigm of communication in general but—more specifically—of commercial communications: based on mutual understanding, with a long-term prospect pointing to a certain seriousness and interest *in each other*.

The significance of marriage as the metaphorical goal to strive for in communications becomes perhaps more evident when we replace marriage with that which precedes it: the engagement. One can engage with any body, any set of bodies. In essence, such an engagement remains asymmetric and we will need to distinguish between the engagement of two people, a trial run of marriage, and the etymological connotations of the word, such as *commit to someone*, but also *"in Sold nehmen"*, *to commit someone* by giving him or her a pay, that is, between an economy of mutual agreement and an economy of asymmetric giving.[138] More than the engagement, marriage is in most cultures the institution for the creation of life, that is, the institution of generation, of generating the gift of life, that which bonds I and Thou together with a responsibility towards future life.

Derrida, in *The Gift of Death*, speaks nowhere clearly of a relation between gift-giving and the responsibility we carry beyond our lives. Only at one point he writes:

> The epilogue of [Kierkegaard's] *Fear and Trembling* repeats, in sentence after sentence, that this highest passion that is faith must be started over by each generation. Each generation must begin again to involve itself in it without counting on the generation before. It thus describes the nonhistory of absolute beginnings which are repeated, and the very historicity that presupposes a tradition of the absolute beginning.[139]

The absolute beginning as the opening of future is based on generation, on the procreation of life, which can never look back but must always be open to conceive a future with the beginning as the point of reference, and marriage is but one metaphor for this duty of generation.

---

138   KLUGE, "Engagement".
139   Derrida, The Gift of Death, 80.

2.3 The habitual

Communis also refers to *allgemein*, to common not only in the strict sense of shared-with, common to all, but also in the sense of ordinary, habitual. It is here that all our previous ruminations may come to a brusque end: if communication refers to the ordinary, how can thinking the extremes of excess, the extremes of symmetry and asymmetry, possibly take into account that which accompanies us every day? Heidegger says on the issue of dwelling and building, which in German go back to the idea of being, that the habitual which we inhabit, the *Gewohnte*, for man's everyday experience "recedes behind the manifold ways in which dwelling is accomplished."[140] To pursue a project of sustainability of communication, we must take into account that which exceeds the fleeting moment, the personal fate, the span of a lifetime; we must move from a particular economy to a general economy—and will likely end up at the habitual again. Let us hear Bataille: "From the *particular* point of view, the problems are posed *in the first instance* by a deficiency of resources. They are posed *in the first instance* by an excess of resources if one starts from the *general* point of view."[141] Although this leaves the vast field of *thinking in the second or third instance* open, it is not at all clear what resource we are talking about. Is there a general resource: a public good, and if so: what is it and for whom? Is the resource of communication not something which only acquires a relevance from a particular point of view, that of scarcity? If it is ordinary in our culture to treat the gift as something which must be topped by a countergift, which in its ever-revolving and ever-expanding cycles heads toward that which cannot be surpassed, must we speak of an economy based on surplus or based on scarcity?

---

140 Heidegger, Basic Writings, 349.
141 Bataille, The Accursed Share, 39.

The economy of human communications and the economy of commercial communications can each be looked at from a general or a particular point of view which cross paths in the notion of freedom of expression where every freedom for one means a different constellation of freedom for the other. The general and particular points of view particularly cross paths within the person of the consumer/citizen: The producer of freckle salve wants to sell his product. In order to do that, if he disposes of the necessary resources (including will), he spends as much as he can afford on a potlatch, an outdoing of the opponent before the very eyes of the public. The currency to humiliate, challenge and obligate[142] the opponent is advertising, which is in itself a free market currency of human attention.[143] The economies of excess and scarcity meet again in the person who has to answer to the accounting department for the extra expenses in the company's economy of scarcity.

2.4   Issues of friendship

So far we have touched upon topics such as the gift and language, which imply further topics such as language, decision, giving, forgiving, responsibility, symmetry and asymmetry, hospitality, death and so on, which can in turn all be grouped under the question of friendship, or more precisely: friendship/enmity, or friend/enemy. In fact, we are tempted to pose all communication as a question of friendship. We have been guided by Derrida's *Politics of Friendship* and *Given Time*, but if we follow his thinking, there is an obstacle to overcome. Even though he makes attempts at criticising the

---

142 Ibid., 67–69.
143 Strangely enough it is rarely the owner of the vision who is paid for what is put in his or her vision.

anthropocentrism inherent in the classical understanding of friendship (this critique mainly being aimed at the issue of non-inclusion of the feminine: sister, daughter, mother[144]), he does state quite clearly that "[f]riendship *par excellence* can only be human" and thinking exists for the human only because it is the thinking of the other as mortal.[145] As we have shown in the first chapter, in commercial communications there is not a mortal being who speaks to us: it is a many-headed organism, everywhere and nowhere simultaneously, latent and manifest in our environment, and the question remains whether such an asymmetric squandering of information, of text in the broad sense, can be likened to human friendship.

Friendship is marked by reciprocity, even if this is never able to cancel out the "infinite" asymmetry. In this it differs from love, where such an asymmetry is not self-evident.[146] It is the reciprocity of the gift and the asymmetry of it, which makes it so difficult to grapple with friendship. Friendship implies so many oppositions that it is uncertain if it is desirable to make a decision, to go with one and deny the other, even to juggle with both: friendship/enmity, giving/receiving, actuality/virtuality, presence/future, life/death. In an infinite movement towards their cancellation, these pairs of oppositions complement each other; in an infinite movement towards their complementation, they cancel each other out.

The concept of the friend implies the concept of the enemy; they are inextricably linked. Schmitt privileges taking the enemy

---

144 This critique is not so much an attack as a search for understanding why there is such an emphasis on fraternity in thinking friendship: "Despite the appearances that this book has multiplied, nothing in it says anything against the brother or against fraternity. No protest, no contestation." Derrida, The Politics of Friendship, 305.

145 Ibid., 224.

146 Ibid., 221. Badiou makes a point in saying that "love begins beyond desire and demand, even if it includes them." Badiou, Wofür steht der Name Sarkozy? 53.

and Derrida the friend as a starting point. The loss of the enemy would not only render the concept of friendship futile, it would also, if we speak of the enemy as political enemy, be the end of politics, according to Schmitt.

2.4.1 Usefulness

Referring to Aristotle's *Eudemian Ethics*, Derrida reports that there are three types of friendship: the first is founded on virtue, the second on usefulness and the third on pleasure.[147] In *Politics of Friendship*, Derrida is primarily interested in the first one. Each of these is further divided into two kinds: those based on equality and those based on difference.[148] If we do not go into further detail as to what this categorisation means in a context where friendship would require humans, we would locate commercial communications that speak to us somewhere between the friendship of usefulness and pleasure, or rather: between usefulness/uselessness and pleasure/pain.

The point of view of usefulness/uselessness might be misunderstood as a positivistic attitude towards progress by pushing the question of whether a piece of information provided by the advertising complex is of use to the receiver or not—and even if it is of no use to anyone, the advertising industry would likely uphold its claim to be the knight for "the rights of the citizen to free information."[149] To measure usefulness would also require a certain measurement for the utility, and here doubtlessly this measure would take on a whole different face if the ruler were politically determined by who sends out or by who receives the message. From a sender's point of view, the usefulness would increase with

---

147 Derrida, The Politics of Friendship, 203.
148 Ibid.
149 Schweizer Werbung SW: Ein Portrait. 8.

every new person an advertisement reaches and with every additional contact an advertisement has with someone it has already made contact with, the sheer number being still a main indicator due to the difficulty of measuring the intensity of mental involvement. Political friendship, i.e. friendship based on utility, is the kind of friendship which allows for a large number of friends, as opposed to friendship based on virtue or pleasure which call for a scarcity of friends. According to Derrida, equality is what political friendship looks to and what concerns it: "As in a market, in commerce between sellers and buyers. Equality and the thing, the equality of things, therefore the third party and the common measure: an account and a fixed wage are necessary: a salary, a fee, a counter-value."[150] We are again faced with an issue of symmetry or balance: is it admissible to say that advertising is a political kind of friendship if such requires equality, equality between a multi-headed, immortal organism and a human person, and if it requires a counter-value, which advertising is not always able to give, and which cannot always be given to advertising?[151] The counter-value that advertising expects from the consumer of the advertisement is attention in the first instance; in the second instance an act of purchase. For such a counter-value, a countergift to take place, the acceptance of the gift—which would annul the gift if we are to follow Derrida—is required. This in turn requires a consciousness

---

150 Derrida, The Politics of Friendship, 204.

151 There is a difference between advertising in a newspaper, where the receiver of the advertisement has a clear financial advantage (newspaper costs $2.50 instead of $15) arising from his consumption of the advertising medium versus billboard advertising or spam, where the receiver has no compensation for the time he or she spends looking at the ad. An often made argument for advertising is that it furthers the production of mass articles at low rates which then benefit the consumers. This may be true in some cases but not all. In an interview with Persönlich, Reto Cina, CEO of Davidoff, claims that his company actually benefits from tobacco advertising bans by saving a lot of marketing money (Persönlich, April 2007. For an abbreviated version, see: http://www.persoenlich.com/news/show_news.cfm?newsid=67510)

towards not only the advert as such but the gift of advertising (get your newspaper for $2.50), in other words the usefulness drawn from exposure to an advertisement—and many market data[152] seem to point to a rather low implicit understanding on behalf of the receiver of these gift-giving mechanisms.[153] Thus we come to the receiver's notion of usefulness of advertising. For him or her, the use value of an advertisement decreases with every new advertisement, because every new one relativises the importance of the former. Even though the probability to find a product which one believes to need is higher with every new advertisement, i.e. an increase of the notion of use value of information, the nature of every new advertisement changes in such a way that the actual value of each piece of information decreases. To summarise: can advertising, leaving aside notions of friendships that only take place between humans, be considered a political type of friendship? From the point of view of who advertises, the answer tends to be yes: more "friends" is better, and the gift to trigger a countergift always takes place (the advertising agency always pays someone to make the advertisement public); what counteracts this is the notion of equality. From the point of view of the receiver, the

---

152   The figure of unaided recalls in outdoor advertising is but one example: "In view of the diversity and multiplicity of information befalling people today, recalls of 2–4% are already considered above-average." (APG Plakatforschung Schweiz. APGTraffic: Fallbeispiel Transport publics de la region lausannoise, 6.) It is to be noted that the APG Affichage, outdoor advertising company with a market share in Switzerland of 75%, is responsible for much of the "diversity and multiplicity" of information. The unaided recall rate depends on the advertisement, the brand, other media involved in the campaign and on the time and place where people are surveyed. Other outdoor advertisers claim a significantly higher unaided recall rate for specific campaigns.

153   Quart points to a strange kind of gift-giving cycle which evolved after 11 Sep 2001, and bridged the consumer, the citizen, the political and the economic realm: all of a sudden, consumption of brandname articles was considered an act of patriotism. This sheds a new light on the understanding of "communication as being-for-others". Quart, Branded, 54f.

answer tends to be no: more "friends" can be counterproductive, the gift is not necessarily accepted, which is why the countergift, the counter-value cannot take place.

2.4.2 Pleasure

If it is only to a limited degree a friendship based on usefulness/ uselessness, in what way can we consider the relationship between a consumer and an advertiser as a friendship based on pleasure/ pain? Derrida does not go to great lengths to explain the circumstances in which such a friendship takes place but he points to the realm of erotic love. To understand what erotic love, pleasurable excitement, means in this context, we may employ André Breton's personal definition as that which, in the act of reception, promptly triggers a bodily excitation, "which makes itself noticed by a spraying and blowing at the temples and may become a genuine shivering."[154] Though the symptoms of this bodily excitation will be different for everyone, it is clear that it need not involve another human person. Erotic love, or rather: asymmetric erotic love, can also be dedicated to an object, a picture, a fetish electrifying the same areas of the brain as that of conventional erotic love of a person: "I have always been incapable of not linking this sensation [Gefühl] to erotic pleasure, and I can only detect gradual differences between the two."[155] With Breton, we arrive at another intersection: that of the German Gefühl, which can take on bodily and mental connotations: feeling, emotion, sensation. It is here where communication economy borders on libidinal economy.

To determine in what way the economic Gefühl relates to "erotic friendship" between humans and non-humans (commercial complexes, objects, advertising messages) would follow much

---

154 Breton, Amour fou. 12.
155 Ibid.

of the same risky paths we took in the ruminations on political friendship:

1) The point of view of advertising: Excitement? Sometimes yes, in the creation of an ad. Singularity of friends? No, the multiplicity suggests friends are not proper friends. Excitement by the friend? There is no friend.

2) The point of view of the spectator: Excitement? Sometimes: "It depends." Singularity of friends? If I have found one, yes. Excitement by the friend? Yes, otherwise it would not be my friend.

To operate with terms that suggest erotic friendship can (might, should) be calculated would enable an economic reading but neutralise what is really at stake and might differ with every reception: the shivering, this uncanny sensation which for a split moment calls into being a glimpse of futurity, the struggle between presence and loss, between excitement and implicit, immediate knowledge that this excitement is going to be gone before it is grasped. It would draw us into the maelstrom of the self-assessment of commercial communications, of utility and not of pleasure, which admittedly, if one is in it deep enough, can cause a sensation of bodily excitement, a sensation which more often than not can be attributed to self-love (being surprised at what one has created or discovered) or to a sense of power.

Even though commercial communications lack certain attributes of a political and erotic friendship (in this respect we have eclipsed friendship based on virtue entirely), we can see how it is still possible to find attributes which would give such a statement some legitimacy. The difficulty arises the moment we have to consider both ends of the communication act, both "friends" to be linked. The asymmetry causes a noise in the reception or acknowledgment of the purported friendship and we can draw no clear line:

The criterion is painfully lacking if we are to judge the just where friendship 'based on usefulness' and friendship 'based on pleasure' end up intersecting in a couple that may very well be called, then, a couple of friends or a couple of lovers. What is lacking at this point is the straight line, the straight and narrow path. When the straight and narrow path does not appear, it becomes difficult to measure the just. This happens with lovers, with 'erotics' when one of them seeks pleasure and the other usefulness. And undoubtedly when the sharing out of these quests becomes equivocal. Everything can function as long as love is there. When love ceases, the two lovers strive to calculate their respective share [...][156]

"When love ceases...": Derrida gives us a criterion whereby to determine the rupture with friendship based on pleasure. In this criterion we recognise that which makes it so difficult to decide whether commercial communications can justly be considered a "friendship" in the sense of pleasure or usefulness. Love, according to Buber, is that which happens *between* the I and the You.[157] The pain of discovering that the usefulness principle has taken over is perhaps the same as the pain Buber hints at when he writes "This however is the sublime melancholy of our lot that every You must become an It in our world."[158] More specifically: that every Thou must *return* to an It.

2.4.3   I, Thou, and being-with

While it is perfectly admissible to define friendship as something which can only take place between humans, it is difficult to maintain this position when talking about communication.

---

156 Derrida, The Politics of Friendship, 205f.
157 Buber, I and Thou, 66.
158 Ibid., 68.

Communication, the manifold instrumentalised term "communication" in everyday language and technical terminology can refer just as much to communication between animals, things and humans, humans and animals, and so on. In *I and Thou*, Buber opposes the relationship of what he calls the primary word I-Thou and the secondary word I-It. What in any case is required is the encounter: "All actual life is encounter."[159] The encounter enables us to turn an It, i.e. the thing-world, that which is latent and waiting to be embosomed by us, into a Thou. The It is necessary to give the Thou a proportion, to bring it into existence, as much as the enemy is necessary to have a perspective of the friend and vice versa. This does not happen by virtue of a mere co-presence: it is our responsibility how much of "the immeasurable becomes reality" for us.[160] Buber determines three spheres "in which the world of relationship is erected": life with nature; life with humans; and life with spiritual beings.[161] Again, we see nowhere a place for such manmade things as advertising unless we decided to give it human (made by humans), natural (made of natural resources), or spiritual (speechless but evoking speech) attributes. We will refrain from doing so as best as we can, but Buber's concept offers valuable insight into communication so it would be unfortunate to dismiss his concept (that which he has conceived), as not applicable simply because it does not materialise in *I and Thou*.

The most significant merit in Buber's thinking is that he does not deny relationships which are not human. According to Buber, we can "communicate"[162] with a tree. If we decide to let the tree be admitted to our world it meets us holistically: in "its form, its mechanics, its colours and its chemistry, its conversation with the

---

159 Ibid., 62.
160 Ibid., 83.
161 Ibid., 56f.
162 "Communicate" is in quotes because Buber does not use the term communications.

elements and its conversation with the stars—all this in its entirety."[163] Once again, it is *us* who are responsible for approaching a being and letting it into our world. It would be problematic to deny those who make an advertisement, a brand, a thing part of their world, who define themselves by the relationship with their objects, the right to enter into such a relationship with these objects, as Buber enters into one with a tree. When he says that the relationship I-Thou is based on natural solidarity while I-It is based on natural detachment,[164] he does not pit the relationship I-Human/Nature/Spirit against the relationship I-Object. What is important is that man makes these objects part of his presence if he or she does not want to be consummated by them: "As [man] accommodates himself to a world of objects that no longer achieve any presence for him, he succumbs to it."[165]

The other significant observation with regard to Buber's three spheres is the copula *with*. (We are still trying to determine whether communication is being-with-others or being-for-others.) He does not only say that we can give the Thou *(das Du geben)*, which is an asymmetric act in itself—one which might not be accepted or perceived at all—he also says that we can receive the Thou.[166] Thus he opens the field of reciprocity which goes beyond the gift tag under the Christmas tree reading "For Pippi" or "For Mister Nilsson" because Buber does not talk about a type of reciprocity which requires the ever-growing countergift.

The *with, mit*, takes us to Heidegger's *Mit-sein* and *Dasein*, a somewhat problematic undertaking as Buber and Heidegger mutually did not seem to heed each other's work.[167] "Buber held that Heidegger's thinking rejects the I-Thou and the realm of the

163   Buber, I and Thou, 58.
164   Ibid., 73.
165   Ibid., 102.
166   Ibid., 57.
167   Gordon, The Heidegger-Buber Controversy, ix–xviii.

interhuman, and, therefore, this thinking lacks an attitude central to human existence", Haim Gordon reports in a study on the status of the I-Thou in Heidegger and Buber.[168] Heidegger's critique of Buber turned this around by rejecting the ontological basis of the I-Thou.[169] Jean-Luc Nancy remarks on the *Mit-sein* of Heidegger's *Dasein* that in *Etre-là Etre-avec* also resonates.[170] Heidegger's idea of Dasein already includes the idea of Mitsein: "Incidentally, *Dasein* is essentially *Mitdasein*. Above all Mitsein is essential to it: A Mit-sein that is not an accumulation of things but an essential Mit."[171] Being-in-the-world is being there with others (the others, according to Heidegger, are those of whom one is not distinct, they are those among whom one is as well). The world is always that which I share with others; the world of Dasein is *Mitwelt*, with-world: "The being-in is being-with-the-others. The inner-worldly *Ansichsein* of the others is *Mitdasein*."[172] It seems there is not a great leap to take between Heidegger and Buber in that being-with is continuously stressed and the criticism addressed at each other appears not always justified. As Gordon remarks, Heidegger is lacking a notion of love, or a notion of "genuine dia-logue",[173] which is central to *I and Thou*. While Heidegger would say that dwelling is building is thinking is being,[174] Buber says that a person dwells in love and feelings dwell in a person.[175] Love, to call it by this name, is the unconditional gift which for Derrida is central to the idea of friendship.

We shall abandon the considerations about differences between Heidegger and Buber at this point in preference for retaining what

168 Ibid., x.
169 Ibid., ix.
170 Nancy, Singulär plural sein, 151.
171 Ibid., 153.
172 Heidegger, Sein und Zeit, 118 (italics mine).
173 Gordon, The Heidegger-Buber Controversy, 116.
174 Heidegger, Basic Writings, 343–364.
175 Gordon, The Heidegger-Buber Controversy, 119.

they share, namely the idea of being-with, the idea that one is never alone in the world. The problem of whether communication, or life or love or being, is essentially being-for or being-with may be answered in the manner that Nancy brought together *Dasein*, *Mitdasein* and *Mitsein*. It is true that the gift, the primary act of giving, is a one-way transmission. It is true that loving is an act of loving *someone* in the first instance, without requiring to be loved back. However, the reaching-out of the being-for can only take place in the interconnectedness of being-with: it requires the other. Being-with always already resonates in being-for. Being-for on the other hand may not necessarily resonate in being-with. It emerges rather as an ethics, perhaps a condition, of being-with. Being-for will thus always hover over true being-with.

If we consider the practice of advertising, we may attest a strong sense of reaching out, but at the same time a weak sense of being-for. In its own conception, in the image the advertising industry is giving itself, there is of course being-for: "we fight *for* the citizen's right to free information" calls forth images of an institution willing to risk its life *for* something the citizen should have a right to. Such a fight would require love but the advertising industry does not love the consumer or the citizen in an interpersonal, ethical way. If it did, not only would it not have to employ bellicose vocabulary; with love, advertising would also not be able to functionally replace one consumer who is unwilling to consume with another one who is not.

Our ruminations so far (but also those of Heidegger, Buber, Derrida and, to a lesser degree, Bataille and Mauss) on being-for and being-with lack a central issue: *the refusal*.[176] A refusal would acknowledge that one is in the same world as that which wants to

---

176   Mauss observes, but leaves it at that: "To refuse to give, to fail to invite, just as to refuse to accept, is tantamount to declaring war; it is to reject the bond of alliance and commonality." Mauss, The Gift, 13.

give or that which is given, for otherwise it would be disregarded or exist in ignorance, but it does not want to be constrained to be-for that which gives or which is given. It does not want to be pressured to be for another being who is *with* and has decided it wants to be *for*. A refusal is a sign that one does not succumb to flexibility.

2.5 Conclusion

The title of the chapter "Communication as being-with-others" was initially changed to "Communication as being-for-others". After the considerations made in this chapter, the working hypothesis that communication is being for others was not generally refuted but it was found that it bears little applicability to the domain of commercial communications—therefore, the title was changed back to "being-with-others". Levinas bears witness to the difficulty of employing either preposition when he mentions in a lecture entitled "Mourir pour..." that he was tempted to change the title to "Mourir ensemble", to die together.[177]

Even though the notions of death, gift and countergift, friend and enemy, and speaking the primary word I-Thou, imply each other and will lead to other notions such as hospitality, host and guest and responsibility, many of them cannot be adapted to the advertising complex. There is a significant lack of involvement and identification on the part of advertising with its target groups; hence notions such as "love", which are essential when speaking of communication in an ethical sense, are not an issue of advertising, even though at times advertising's self-assessment claims that this is true in some way. The lack of love or identification in this case does not imply the opposite, hatred or conscious indifference, it is

---

177   Levinas, in: Lesch, "Fragmente einer Theorie der Gerechtigkeit", 172.

simply a category unsuited for commercial communications if we accept advertising as something coming from a multi-bodied entity, which is not animated the way a human is. Though one might love something inanimate, Derrida claims that "loving belongs only to a being gifted with life or with breath."[178]

This deficit can, on the one hand, be attributed to the functional exchangeability of consumers in the eyes of commercial communications—and vice versa. On the other hand, it can be attributed to the technical makeup of advertising channels, which in today's practice are largely one-way channels. While it is true that love is asymmetric in the first place, this condition is not enough to speak of love.

It still proves useful to think of advertising as embedded in a general economy of overabundance. Advertising can be a gift but it is a gift in a paradoxical way. The gift, according to Derrida, must be disinterested and unrecognised. Though it is true that there is a certain disinterest by advertising in the consumer as a singular, irreplaceable person, advertising is heavily vested with interest: it seeks—often in vain—to be recognised. Since it is vested with interest, it is not perceived as a gift but as a deal, an agreement, a contract. It fulfils one of the conditions of a gift while the other condition is somewhat ambiguous. But, again paradoxically, the unrecognised gift still hopes for a countergift: the purchase of the advertised product or service.

Since "being-for" does not seem applicable to the advertising complex, even though it reaches out, we followed the idea of communication as "being-with", which leads us to consider the natural sphere as a rhizome of an infinite number of—at least in a virtual way—interconnected nodes. The rhizome follows the paradigm of distributed balance, a continuing struggle between symmetric and asymmetric communication. It requires us to live in a state of openness, of letting be and letting go.

---

178   Derrida, The Politics of Friendship, 12.

3 Communication as life

In the introduction to the chapter on advertising we hinted at the fact that the anthropocentric use of the term "communication" dominates in everyday language. Most thinkers we quoted thus far conceal that their thinking might bear relevance to non-human communication. Even Buber, who seems closest to understanding communication as something which does not necessarily need to take place between two persons, does not talk about the possibility of two non-natural or non-human entities communicating. We recall the three spheres of establishing a relationship, according to Buber: life with nature; life with humans; and life with spiritual beings.[179] "Life with" could refer to any life but in what follows, he implicitly understands these relationships as between human and nature, human and human, and human and spiritual being.

This view of communication is sufficient for many applications and theories but it is too limited for a broad understanding of communication. For instance, it bypasses biosemiotic theories where the communicants may not even be in physical proximity and do not dispose of communication channels intelligible or discernible to the human mind. It also does not describe biological reproduction, the transmission of energy or pandemics. And lastly, it is limited in understanding communication issued from commercial organisms where the singular human disappears.

---

179 Buber, I and Thou, 56f.

Although Buber displays sensitivity towards the infinite rhizome of relationships, there is a certain risk that an anthropocentric focus may also lead to an anthropocentric application without a perspective on the other beings' life-force or *generans*. This is what Günter Altner refers to when he claims that "The peculiar anthropocentrism of the modern perception should be busted like a dangerously restrictive carapace or armour *(Panzer)* and be superseded by an open perspective of 'co-creatureness' *(Mitkreatürlichkeit)*."[180] This co-creatureness he summarises in the formula "I am life that wants to live in the midst of life that wants to live."[181] He calls for a broadening of human rights to living rights.[182] Altner seems to bear in mind in the first place natural living organisms. When he speaks about the soul life of plants and, generally, of living organisms, he has in mind the "plants' genuine life capacity they fulfil in the great history of becoming and passing away of nature."[183]

3.1 Zoé and bios

A notion of general communications must take into account everything that is present, even without our knowledge, everything that is breathing, pulsating, growing, moving, changing, even that to which we ordinarily do not attribute a consciousness. We live as environment; we are bios from the start, Schirmacher notes.[184] One can argue that we are *zoon* from the start, that is, bare life. Giorgio Agamben reports that *zoé* means the mere fact of life, that which is common to all living, and *bios* means the individual way

---

180   Altner, in: Zum Naturbegriff der Gegenwart, 262.
181   Ibid., 274.
182   Ibid., 262.
183   Ibid., 266f.
184   Schirmacher, Ethik im Horizont der Künstlichkeit.

of living of someone or a group.[185] As such, *zoé/bios* is, according to Agamben, the fundamental pair of categories of the political, and not friend/enemy: "Politics exist because man is the living being that separates bare life from itself in language and opposes it to itself and at the same time maintains the relationship to it by an inclusive exclusion."[186] The fact of being born and cast into this world is what we share in the first place with all living being while the socialisation, the individual biography, the lifelong search for a good life in a community, even if this community is just a community with the elements, in short: politics, is what we can only gradually acquire during our stay.

On the level of bare life, all that lives is equal in that it lives. If there exists such a right as the right to live, something we should at least for the moment be suspicious of, it is to be located on this level. By saying that we should be suspicious of such a right we do not deny that many legal systems are based on this notion or that life is worth preserving. It is rather that "right" already implies a human concept: "Man himself was their source as well as their ultimate goal", Arendt remarks on the Rights of Man at the end of the eighteenth century, which was hardly different with the 1948 declaration of human rights.[187] Natural rights cannot be prior to man, prior to socialisation or society at large and still incorporate cultural and moral values since the only common denominator of living beings, even a subset of living beings such as humanity, is that they are equal in that they live. One might therefore rather say that it is a natural *law* that all that lives is equal in that it lives. Schirmacher implies a natural right when he claims that no one is entitled to touch

---

185   Agamben, Mittel ohne Zweck, 13.
186   Agamben, Homo Sacer, 18.
187   Arendt, The Portable Hannah Arendt, 31. The chapter "The Perplexities
      of the Rights of Man" in the Arendt reader, taken from *The Origins of
      Totalitarianism*, is a lucid critique of the notion and institution of human
      rights.

the rights of living creatures.[188] He does not substantiate what kind of rights these might be but it is sufficiently clear that he does not refer to a number of certain rights living creatures may be granted but to the very basic right to live. In view of the natural cycles which are based on consumption of living matter it has an aftertaste of an ethical right: a right of and for well-meaning *people*. Schirmacher exempts the act of self-defence *(Notwehrrecht)* for *our* genus from his concept of a "natural right".[189] This is a somewhat problematic undertaking. Even though our perspective on nature can always only be a human perspective, and even though the notion of natural law paradoxically does not aim at nature but at humanity, "*our* genus" is a limited anthropocentric focus. In the context of the article quoted from (animal experiments), this perspective may be granted but in any general system (economy, ecology, communication), it needs to open up to self-defence of *any species* if it is not to lead to a subjugation of nature. What is at stake in the biological sphere as well as in the human sphere is the uniqueness of the irreplaceable other. To kill amounts to extinguishing the unique other and depriving the world of that particular uniqueness. Rosalyn Diprose reads Levinas with reference to the uniqueness of the other:

> What Levinas does say is that this expression of uniqueness of the other puts existence on a human and moral plane; it says 'thou shalt not kill' and this unique sense starts the circulation of meaning that constitutes responsibility and community. As a response to the other's finitude I am therefore responsible for the other who moves me and who I cannot contain (although Levinas sometimes extends this responsibility for the other further by saying that I am 'responsible for what they do or suffer').[190]

---

188 Schirmacher, Ethik im Horizont der Künstlichkeit.
189 Ibid.
190 Diprose, Responsibility in a Place and Time of Terror, §23.

The riddle to resolve is whether non-unique beings, or at least, replaceable beings—such as advertisements that may be replaced by other, for our perception identical, advertisements—are to be granted the same rights to live. What in any case can be said is that, if we follow Levinas, this uniqueness is the basis for community and for responsibility within and reaching out of this community. "Thou shalt not kill" is the life-affirming command that puts our responsibility as well as our own life into the perspective of the irreplaceable. If everyone is responsible for the unique other, we cannot claim to be innocent; the responsibility for the life of the other as unique generating force driving towards the immediate start of the future cannot be declined.

A note on "innocent" life: I was always struck by the use of the term "innocent life".[191] The killing of "innocent life" is never caused by an accident or a natural catastrophe but always by an assassin of sorts and it appears to come up more often when a relatively large number of people are killed. The rhetoric of "innocent life" presupposes that there is such a thing as "guilty" life. The story dates back to the New Testament (John 8:7: who is without sin shall cast the first stone). Its implications have been turned around and only the universality of the example retained.[192] In the Bible, Jesus presupposes not only that there is sinful life but that all life is sinful while today's media rhetoric presupposes that the normal life is innocent and guilt can only be attributed to someone attacking this innocent standard life. Both points are difficult

---

191 In a short essay entitled "Der Zorn der Verdammten" (The wrath of the damned), Orhan Pamuk uses the term "innocent life" to such a degree that it almost becomes a mantra. Pamuk, Der Blick aus meinem Fenster, 52–57. Pamuk also wrote a book entitled *The Museum of Innocence* and would like to build an actual museum by that name.

192 We would be faced with a whole different story if just one drunkard in the lynching mob had not heeded the words of Jesus and thrown the first stone whereupon it is likely that the mob would have stoned the woman they considered a sinner.

to defend—not the least because they suppose a universality of values. Not only is sin always defined by religion and guilt by the law (which might take religion as a starting point), who in turn shape what (in Heidegger's sense) *man*, they, think: the moral sets of values of a culture. Who does not belong to a specific culture or religion will likely not share all these moral values—thus there can be no strict universality (after all, the human rights were not "universal" before their declaration on 10 December 1948).[193] It further does not take into account the possibility that one's sins might be washed away by a however worldly or religious confession or by undoing the damages, if such is at all possible. One could therefore rather argue that no life is guilty, or, to resolve this aporia, that guilty/not guilty, sinful/not sinful, are oppositions which are not applicable to life and which must be replaced by the opposition, in itself no less problematic, of responsible/not responsible.

Since all beings that are part of the combustive cycles of the natural sphere rely on consumption of others, there is a limit to the command of not killing. In the end, "ethical" killing boils down to eating. Bataille held that eating meat was a luxury of nature, a squandering of energy to be consumed—consummated—lustfully. [194] Schirmacher somewhat enigmatically calls for an autarchic species of artificial beings (i.e. mankind) that would not have to kill to stay alive but would be "carried by total nature" (*Gesamtnatur*).[195] Two interpretations of this ability to be "carried by nature as a whole" can be offered: 1) Schirmacher envisions a new human species which defies the most basic law of nature, that of consumption. 2) He envisions a way of life, which, along the lines of Michael Braungart and William A. McDonough's efforts working with the producing industry, gives back the matter

---

193   Universal Declaration of Human Rights.
194   Bataille, The Accursed Share, 33.
195   Schirmacher, Die Provokation der Gentechnologie.

it extracted—in an uncontaminated way. The latter interpretation views killing as something which has no impact on the general system. The framework in which we live has two determinants: mass (the planet earth) and energy (the sun). Since the biomass on the planet remains the same, with the exception of the occasional meteorite shower, and only energy is added by means of sunlight, life is always at the expense of other life. Even in mental creation that appears to be a creation out of nothingness, there is biomass involved and it is only due to the microscopic scale of mental processes that we believe that mental creation does not kill another creation. The expansiveness of one creation may not only kill off what is needed to feed on, it might also prevent generation of new creation.

Offensive and defensive self-defence seem to tell the story of the survival of the strongest, but this story is in itself corrupted. Strength is to be looked at in terms of fitness, which is to be seen in proportion to the environment, which, especially when dominated by manmade technology, may change more rapidly than non-technological beings can adapt their genetic traits. While the bare human is perhaps the weakest and not the fittest, thanks to technology, it becomes the fittest, so fit that the extermination not only of others but of the human species itself is at stake. Instrumental technology might thus lead to a self-extermination of the fittest and everything else. On the brighter side, the "strongest" might very well be able to coexist with the "weaker". It is not the strongest who survive but those best adapted who prosper: "[I]n healthy and functioning natural systems it is basically the best adapted which prospers. Adaptation means an energetic and material connection with the location and a mutual relationship with it."[196]

Each species needs its niche. Only multiplicity seems to guarantee that life continues indefinitely. We therefore are to contribute to a general framework which sets the conditions for an

---

196 Braungart and McDonough, Einfach intelligent produzieren, 155.

indefinite and infinite generation of matter and ideas. We cannot shut down or kill a node in the rhizome of life because we cannot estimate the consequences of it. The moment we kill something, we deprive it not only of the capacity to generate itself; we also deprive all the other nodes of the possibility to generate something in interaction with what we have killed.

3.2   Between birth and death

The eternal becoming and passing away of all living things oscillate between natality and mortality, between birth and death, where birth always means destined for death and death always means giving place to new birth. This view differs of course from Arendt when she says that "mortality as such is a distinguish mark of human existence" and that humans are different from other living beings in that their life is linear and not inscribed into a biological cycle.[197] In her discussion of infinity and immortality, she is able to make this claim taking recourse to the concept of language, which many agree is the actual distinguishing mark of humans.[198] Although we can disagree with Arendt when she exempts mankind from the cycles biological beings are subjected to, we should recognise the importance of her observation that there is an urge in humans to acquire a specific kind of immortality—a human immortality—by having a recognisable biography and by bringing forth works, deeds, and words.[199]

---

197   Arendt, Vita activa, 29.
198   Sebeok, Global Semiotics, 29 ("[A]nthroposemiosic component, which necessarily and additionally implicates language"); Schirmacher, Culture Between Conformity and Resistance ("The human individual is a cultural being that with the aid of linguistic symbols creates a world not provided for by nature.").
199   Arendt, Vita activa, 29.

"Natality and mortality do not mark beginning and end of the human individual; they are instead the existential techniques generating our entire lives," Schirmacher states.[200] By tuning out of these natural cycles we become estranged to our natural habitat, as little as there might remain. Only if we let these other creatures, the weeds, critters, bacteria, water, air, celestial bodies, come into our lives, if we accept them as equally struggling for a good life, do we find our dwelling place "on the earth, under the sky, before the divinities."[201] Only when we attribute something like a soul to our fellow beings will we be able to speak the primary word I-Thou.[202] Communication, or life in general, must be practiced as an activity "from cradle to cradle" and not "from the cradle to the grave".[203] It must give back what is borrowed.

Bataille's observations on the economy of excess are firmly grounded in nature's exuberant productivity. He speaks of a natural limit to growth, the turning point where energy must be luxuriously dissipated. Though it is true that singular bodies physically cannot grow indefinitely because they would diminish the other's ability to grow, they can very well grow in a metaphysical sense until death puts an end to the function of the organs responsible for growth and the maintenance of a particular life. At one point, Bataille insists that "there is generally no growth but only a luxurious squandering of energy in every form!"[204] If that is the case, then the opposite may also be the case: there is no squandering of energy but only growth. Since the mass remains constant and only energy is added, growth can only be conceived either as singular growth, that is the growth of a singular body or a species at the expense of other growth, or as a metaphysical kind of growth, a

200 Schirmacher, Net Culture.
201 Heidegger, Basic Writings, 352.
202 Buber, I and Thou.
203 Braungart and McDonough, Einfach intelligent produzieren.
204 Bataille, The Accursed Share, 33. Exclamation mark his.

growth—for the lack of a better term—in organic intelligence or energetic intelligence. We imagine the sphere of general communications as a rhizome with an infinite number of nodes and an infinite number of connections between these nodes—from our neural nets to the cosmos, the universal interrelatedness *("universeller Lebenszusammenhang").*[205] Jean-François Lyotard writes (about humans): "The self is little, but it is not isolated, it is caught in a structure of relations, which has never been as complex and mobile as it is today... It is always set on 'nodes' of a communication circuitry, as insignificant as they may be."[206] Similarly, Flusser argues that we are nodes of relationships that only become real in relation to others. Thus, the stronger the relationship, the closer someone is connected to me, and I to him or her, and the more intense the information transmission.[207] Flusser also submits this concept to an anthropology, but in views of the brain and other rhizomatic organisms, this particular viewpoint is limited. The rhizome connects all bodies—past, present, and future; bodies of humans, animals, plants, text, machines. Without the net or the rhizome there is no relationship. Being-with lies down the infrastructure in which being-for may take place. In Alain Badiou's words: "Before one can worry about 'quality of life', as the well-fed citizens of the protected world do, one has to live, like billions of human animals struggle to do—elsewhere, and increasingly here as well."[208] The question of existence precedes the question of quality.

When we consider communication as life, it is useful to look at achievements in the field of semiotics. In the past forty years, semiotics started to focus on the entire planet, if not the universe, and discovered and coined a number of highly interesting modes of communication all across the biosphere. Thomas A. Sebeok, one

---

205   Schirmacher, Die Provokation der Gentechnologie.
206   Lyotard, Das postmoderne Wissen, 55.
207   Flusser, Medienkultur, 146f.
208   Badiou, Wofür steht der Name Sarkozy? 58.

of the pioneers, following Jakob von Uexküll, claims that "[t]he province of biosemiotics coincides in its entirety with that of the biosphere, which, in this context, is tantamount to the 'semiosphere'."[209] Thus, bios = sign; life = communication. He proposes two axioms of semiotics: 1) The criterial mark of all life is semiosis;[210] 2) semiosis presupposes life.[211] Sebeok does not exactly explain how this is to be applied to the inanimate components of the biosphere ("the lithosphere, the hydrosphere, and the atmosphere, each being a compound component of a global unitary autopoiesis, i.e., a homeostatic self-regulation system"[212]), which, according to him, is the playground for "universal" semiotics. He however makes a point in that it is messages (DNA) which connect us to the past.[213] Adherents to the diverse biosemiotic theories locate communication in the five superkingdoms: protists, bacteria, plants, animals and fungi.[214] The bacterial superkingdom is the most encompassing communication network of all:

> According to the modern view of semiosis in the microcosmos, or bacterial semiosis, all bacteria on Earth constitute the communications network of a single superorganism whose continually shifting components are dispersed across the surface of the planet.[215]

The human is part of the animal superkingdom, which is characterised by an in-between position between the "phytosemiotic and the mycosemiotic operations", that is, we are mediators between

---

209 Sebeok, Global Semiotics, 33.
210 Sebeok refers to both Peirce's usage of semiosis as "action of a sign" and to Morris' definition as semiosis as "a sign-process, that is, a process in which something is a sign to some organism" (Ibid., 17).
211 Ibid., 10.
212 Ibid., 11.
213 Ibid., 19.
214 Ibid., 23.
215 Ibid., 23.

creation and decay.[216] This honourable role between birth and birth, the role of a facilitator of creation has been neglected by the industrial revolution which viewed nature as a threat and which has had a major impact on our thinking (that is, building, dwelling, living) to such an extent that humanity has not facilitated decay, which consequently leads to new life, but created a number of substances that do not break down in due time. The industrial revolution is thus marked by hubris of man over nature, a hubris which prefers short-term manageable monoculture over long-term diversity which cannot entirely be grasped or tended.

The megalomania of the industrial revolution, the image of nature as a threat rather than an origin, can also be diagnosed in today's practice of advertising, where nature of course takes on a different shape. The natural environment of advertising is the rhizome of human-generated meaning with reference to purchasable products and services. The diversity of advertising messages is celebrated only within the advertising complex ("together we stand, divided we fall"), often under the guise of providing information to the citizen/consumer, but never in particular advertising where another advertising message is considered a threat since it diminishes the citizen/consumer's attention devoted to the message. Again, particular and general advertising can be linked to particular and general economy in that the particular systems are ruled by scarcity and the general systems by abundance.

The chaotic, unpredictable nature of acts taking place in the great rhizome (and nothing is outside it), the grand narrative of chaos theory, leaves us with the ethical and logical imperative of a humbleness towards our own actions and those of others. It leaves us as much with a sense of fatality as with a sense of responsibility; with a sense of fatality of our responsibility as with a sense of responsibility for the fatality, which can perhaps best be faced in

---

216   Ibid., 42.

a state of equanimity, of letting go, of *Gelassenheit*. Derrida links responsibility to faith and the gift of death, which would be the "marriage" of the former two.[217] It is precisely that which exceeds knowledge (faith, chaos), the undecidable, which marks responsibility:[218] "[I]f decision-making is relegated to a knowledge that it is content to follow or to develop, then it is no more a responsible decision, it is the technical deployment of a cognitive apparatus, the simple mechanistic deployment of a theorem."[219] This is the reason why neurologists, who have a fundamental understanding of the brain as a mechanistic apparatus, where a cause has an effect, where an effect is caused, often claim there is no free will and, consequently, there can be no responsibility. If all can be explained and nothing is undecidable, responsibility can only be attributed as a mechanistic concept. Since, however, this is not the case—and there is little use assuming it might one day be—we are faced with the challenge of responsibility and humility.

3.3　Ambiguities in artificial life

The considerations on natural life as the sphere of communication lay down the traces that we are to follow, but that we must expand in order to justify the pervasiveness of communication. If people, especially young people in the Western hemisphere, today know thousands of brand names but not even twenty wildflowers,[220] it is a sign of a shift in the perception of our environment. The

---

217 Derrida, The Gift of Death, 6.
218 Ibid., 5.
219 Ibid., 24.
220 This study has been mentioned several times to me but I have not been able trace it. We shall thus treat it as an indicative anecdote. This does not only appear to be applicable to animals. A friend of mine reported that when he goes for jogs in the forest, he can hear birds imitating cell-phone ring tones.

knowledge of wildflowers is not as decisive for survival and navigation in our culture as that of brand names. Wildflowers are not as omnipresent as brand names. The difference between wildflowers and brands is of course that brands give themselves a meaning whereas wildflowers are only given a meaning by an outside spectator.

Commercial messages (including brands *per sé*) must somehow be separated from the sender because, as we have seen in the first chapter, there is not a singular natural being who issues many of these messages and the message itself, any message, when it emanates from the sender also emancipates itself. It becomes a piece of the world to be grabbed or disregarded. These pieces of the world are artificial; they are part of a "world not provided for by nature."[221]

Or are they? If mankind is part of nature, if a human being is *zoé* in the first place, how can anything the human sets into the world be outside nature? Is the complex communicative system of a beehive or an anthill artificial or natural? In their industrial concept of cradle-to-cradle, which is limited to biological cycles, Braungart and McDonough distinguish between biological and technical metabolisms.[222] They claim that these two domains cannot be mingled without mutually diminishing the other's quality in the process of disintegration. For our argument it is useful to augment the biological and technical metabolisms by another—albeit non-physical—metabolism: the language metabolism. Despite the appeal to treat humans as part of the animal kingdom, Sebeok concedes that it is language in which mankind differs from other animals: "The term zoosemiotics […] denotes semiosis in animals inclusive of the nonverbal semiosic component in man, in contrast to the anthroposemiosic component, which necessarily and

---

221   Schirmacher, Net Culture.
222   Braungart and McDonough, 136f.

additionally implicates language."[223] If we follow Schirmacher, it is indeed the linguistic system which is responsible for our particular modes of behaviour, of generation of meaning—which encompass also our mastery of the technical metabolism: "The human individual is a cultural being that with the aid of linguistic symbols creates a world not provided for by nature."[224] This definition requires further specification if it is to separate the cultural achievements of mankind from that of other animals. "The human being separates itself from raw perception, from the experience of *hic et nunc*, with the aid of the sign," Umberto Eco states.[225] The same can however be said of the bee's dance, where a bee is thought to indicate the location of a feeding site by the pattern of its dance.[226] When a dog marks his territory and another dog walks past, it signals that this is the former dog's territory *hic et nunc* even though it is not present anymore.

Nevertheless, we will for the moment follow both Eco's exclusion of the animal and plant sphere[227] and Schirmacher's definition of artificial as human-created[228] in order to treat messages that do not issue from a specific human being as stand-alone entities in the rhizome of general communications, something Sebeok implies he agrees with when he augments the area of semiosis as that of living things by "man's inert extensions, such as automata, computers, or robots."[229] "Computers and robots" is not to say that we are in the realm of virtual reality; there is a net difference between the virtual and the artificial: "'Virtual reality' simulates reality by creating a 'double world' in which new possibilities may

223 Sebeok, Global Semiotics, 27.
224 Schirmacher, Net Culture.
225 Eco, Zeichen: Einführung in einen Begriff und seine Geschichte. 108
226 ScienceDaily, Waggle dance controversy resolved by radar records of bee flights.
227 Eco, Zeichen. Einführung in einen Begriff, 37.
228 Schirmacher, Homo Generator: Media and Postmodern Technology.
229 Sebeok, Global Semiotics, 37.

be explored" while "artificial life describes the only life we know anything about: humanity."[230] "Artificial" does not denote "fake" because artificial life does not imitate life. If "virtual" only creates a double world, it can be considered fake. If, however, the virtual world is one "in which new possibilities may be explored" it is genuine.

Following Schirmacher, it seems that humanity does not distinguish itself from other forms of life in that it lives an artificial life ("the only world we know anything about"), if we broaden the horizon to apply the basic idea of artificial life to any being. If artificial life is the term for the only thing a species can grasp since it is the only world it knows, we only have to exclude the human to see that other beings can be leading artificial lives as well: the bee's communication (the dance) would still be artificial life for the bee since it is the only form of life the bee knows anything about. There are species but nature does not know or distinguish them. Humanity appears as the species capable of creating a virtual reality thanks to language. Even then, the "sharp distinction" Schirmacher makes between virtual and artificial is in fact not that sharp, or in any case not mutually exclusive, because artificial life is by definition the starting point for the creation of a virtual reality: "We could not have discovered gene technology or virtual reality as human capability if it did not belong to our nature and if it were not a characteristic of our life technology."[231] This view contrasts with what Jean-Luc Nancy claimed, namely that humans differ from other forms of life in that they are able to generate things that exceed the predetermined code of nature.[232] Bees seem only able to build beehives in a certain way whereas humans seem to have at disposal infinite possibilities of building habitations.

---

230   Schirmacher, Homo Generator: Media and Postmodern Technology.
231   Ibid.
232   Nancy, personal communication, 11 June 2007.

Thus, if these infinite possibilities are engraved in our nature, we are in this respect not any different from other living beings.

The merit of a concept of artificial life is that it extends this type of life to "humanity" and not necessarily to a singular human being. Thus, whatever takes place in the human world may be regarded as originating in artificial life. The parallels we drew in the first chapter between natural persons and juristic persons cannot be subsumed in that the juristic person is a fake, imitating the natural person.[233] With the concept of artificial life we have something at hand which remains on the horizon of human perception yet which in many ways goes beyond the natural world as the habitat, however "artificial", of humanity.

What we learn from this is that we are to treat messengers as messages and vice versa, but not in an undifferentiated way of simply reiterating what in its catchy form has become a dictum: that the medium is the message.[234] Rather, the rhizome of general communications connects in a virtual way ("virtual" in the sense of not necessarily actualised at the moment of examination) all heterogeneous nodes. Since they are heterogeneous singularities, we need to discriminate in a positive sense. A billboard cannot be compared to a bee or a human but it has its place in the rhizome of general communications nevertheless, a place that however may be argued in that it is an inert, repeatable object which still may occupy unique living things such as brain cells. Its uniqueness derives only from the uniqueness of a situation it offers the spectator.

---

233 It is merely the self-image of a company that draws analogies between a natural organism and the commercial organism. Most often, companies grow organically and it is only in retrospect that we liken the artificial construct to a natural one.

234 McLuhan, Understanding Media, 7ff. McLuhan was much more differentiated: "'message' of any medium or technology is the change of scale or pace or pattern that it introduces into human affairs" (8); "'the medium is the message' because it is the medium that shapes and controls the scale and form of human association and action." (9).

Not only do we need to discriminate between the nature (or make-up) of the messengers and the messages (as much as we need to take into account the intended or potential host ("receiver of guests") of the message). We also need to discriminate between communication acts by their weight and vector, which can be understood as the closeness of the relationship between two nodes or, in Flusser's words, the number of threads that link two nodes and thus the amount of information that is exchanged between them.[235]

3.4   Balance as the paradigm of communication

We have dedicated a good deal of time to the question whether communication is symmetric or asymmetric and we recall that the former implies an exchange of information (or of gifts in the broad sense) whereas the latter refers to a transmission, which as such can be considered a subset of the symmetric concept of communication. The considerations that followed pointed towards a more ethical approach of the point of view of communication as something asymmetric while the concept of symmetric communications implied a closed systemic view of sorts. We still keep in mind that there are communication acts specifically programmed in such a way that they must remain asymmetric: the ultimate gift, billboards, spam, viruses. When we are urged to discriminate between different messengers and messages, the question of the degree of symmetry plays a decisive role. Since asymmetry implies a lack or a defect in symmetry, and vice versa, we should thus work with the term "balance" instead:

---

235   Flusser, Medienkultur, 146.

The substance whose entire, not presupposed substantiality consists in touching other substances: declination of atoms, mutual weighing, and/or networks, infections, communications of the "This", other modes of weighing. Weighing: creation. That with which creation begins without presupposing a creator. Subject that was there before any other subject, weighing, exercised, received drive, fully archiprimitive community of forces, bodies as forces, forms of bodies—psyches—as forces that push each other, support each other, repel, modify each other, combine, rise in each other. The weights share out the expansiveness, extensions and contractions.[236]

Balance, symbol of *iustitia*[237], means equilibrium and originates from the late Latin term "bilanx", which meant two shells *(Schale, Waagschale)* of a scale *(Waage)*.[238] Balance should not be read as eternal and static—least of all in a particular communication situation. Rather, it implies the *search* for equilibrium, the eternal contestation, the game and the countergame. The search for balance is also the issue of hospitality.[239] On a classic weighing machine we do not know how much the contents of one scale weigh if they are not balanced by the other scale.[240] "To be weighed," Nancy tells us, "requires the help of another body and the expansiveness

236 Nancy, Corpus, 84.
237 The balance is one symbol for justice. The other symbol, the symbol for juridical justice, as the online resource *Das grosse Kunstlexikon von W. P. Hartmann* informs us, is the sword, which takes us back to the scission and the de-scission again. Das grosse Kunstlexikon von W. P. Hartmann, "Justitia".
238 KLUGE, "Balance".
239 The Latin word for equalize or compensate is "hostire", which has the same root as hospitality and hostility. Georges, Lateinisch-Deutsches Wörterbuch.
240 The difficulty for a German native speaker is that the two parts (two scales, *zwei Schalen*) make up the whole (the scale, *die Waage*). To avoid misunderstandings, I therefore use weighing machine. At the same time, balance is the thing *(Waage)* as well as its predicate, or rather, the predicate it aims at.

of the world."[241] When the weighing machine is in balance, it is only in balance by virtue of its approximate character and the friction between its parts. It is unlikely that in the practical world two things exist that weigh exactly the same.[242] The difference in weight between the two scales *(Schalen)* can only be determined by adjusting the scale *(Waage)* infinitely more accurately and counterbalance that which is heavier. Balance may thus be likened to the idea of consensus. Consensus is not a fixed state, an eternal harmony of judgments; it is not even justice,[243] let alone truth.[244] It is rather "a condition of the discussion and not its goal."[245] Derrida teaches us that "'good friendship' supposes disproportion. It demands a certain rupture in reciprocity or equality, as well as the interruption of all fusion or confusion between you and me."[246] As such, good friendship need not be based on consensus but on asymmetric giving. This however does not imply that the asymmetry is one-sided. While love requires only an object to be loved, friendship requires two objects and two subjects, both of which are treated as irreplaceable singularities to whom we give without asking for something in return. Friendship is thus two-sided asymmetry. Lesch writes that "in the inequality [Ungleichheit] of my relationship to the other [...] the call for justice is already embedded, though not in the sense of a reciprocally-egalitarian relationship but as a correction of this asymmetry."[247]

---

241 Nancy, Corpus, 82.
242 We use the term "practical world" because it is believed that atoms of the same element have the same atomic weight.
243 Lyotard, Das Postmoderne Wissen, 190.
244 In a seminar in Saas-Fee in August 2006, Žižek claimed: "Truth isn't in the balance. To strike a balance and call it truth is obscene. Truth is not equal with adequacy." (transcription mine).
245 Lyotard, Das postmoderne Wissen, 190.
246 Derrida, The Politics of Friendship, 62.
247 Lesch, W. "Fragmente einer Theorie der Gerechtigkeit", 185f.

Balance implies a back-and-forth, which is beautifully described by a speculation in the KLUGE Etymologisches Wörterbuch: "The prefix *bal-* instead of *bil-* may rest on secondary motivation, such as the late Latin *ballāre*, to dance, to move."[248] KLUGE also reminds us that balance is often used in connection to tightrope walking. We cannot think of dance without recalling its greatest advocate, Nietzsche. Zarathustra, the man who walks like a dancer[249] speaks: "Cease not your dancing, you lovely maidens! [...] How could I, you light-footed ones, be hostile to divine dances?"[250] Dance is the eternal contestation, the elusive (note the playful, *ludere*), the state where balance is never achieved (thus not a state in the strict sense), the ecstatic back-and-forth. Badiou writes that dance resists the "great enemy of Zarathustra-Nietzsche, the enemy he names 'the ghost of gravity' [Geist der Schwere]. The dance emblematises in the first place a kind of thinking that withdraws from the ghost of gravity."[251]

This contestation implies the necessary danger of a life in search for balance. We recall the equilibrist in Zarathustra who is suddenly taken over by a harlequin, a buffoon, which brings him out of balance and causes his deadly fall. Before dying, the equilibrist looks up to Zarathustra kneeling beside him and speaks: "I am not much more than an animal which has been taught to dance by blows and a few scraps of food."—"Not at all," said Zarathustra, "you have made danger your calling; there is nothing contemptible in that. Now you perish by your calling: therefore I will bury

---

248 KLUGE, "Balance". The etymology of *Tanz*, dance, according to KLUGE, is uncertain. It is thought to go back to *de-antiare*, move ahead.

249 Nietzsche, Also sprach Zarathustra, 60. Note: while the page numbers refer to the German edition (see bibliography), the translations are, for the sake of convenience, taken from the online source http://users.telenet.be/sterf/texts/phil/Nietzsche-ThusSpokeZarathustra.pdf, a translation by Thomas Common, edited by Paul Douglas.

250 Nietzsche, Also sprach Zarathustra, 135.

251 Badiou, Kleines Handbuch der In-Ästhetik, 79.

you with my own hands."[252] Dance is danger. Dance is ecstasy, being outside oneself. The dancing body speaks out from within itself,[253] but it is not the freed bodily impulse, the untamed bodily energy that Nietzsche would call vulgarity [Gemeinheit].[254] "It rather shows us on a bodily level the *insubordination* against the impulse. [...] One must understand lightness as the ability of the body to express itself as an uncoerced body, also towards itself, that is, a body that does not obey its impulses."[255] Whenever one is outside oneself, one lives on a string, like the equilibrist, one puts one's life in danger—albeit in a rewarding way if one masters the art of dancing:

> Smooth ice
> Is paradise
> For those who dance with expertise.[256]

The danger inherent in the idea of balance is two-fold. The first danger is that in a particular system a certain balance is achieved that turns the system into an inert entity, which is so obsessed with staying in balance, or which has parts that cause so much friction that it is not able to behave dynamically in a general system. The other danger is that a particular system is so out of balance that it either dominates other particular systems or that it collapses entirely. An idea of balance must be able to take into account interplay if it is to remain constant but not rigid, if its balance is to be sustainable. Watzlawick *et al.* stressed that symmetric and complementary forms of relationship mutually stabilise each other.[257] The

---

252 Nietzsche, Also sprach Zarathustra, 67.
253 Badiou, Kleines Handbuch der In-Ästhetik, 80.
254 Ibid., 82.
255 Ibid., 83.
256 Nietzsche, Gay Science, §13.
257 Watzlawick, Beavin and Jackson, Menschliche Kommunikation, 103–113.

singular nodes in the great rhizome must be sufficiently dynamic or, rather, plastic to distribute the particular inequalities or imbalances in such a way that they together, if not knowingly, work towards a relatively stable but never inert or rigid general system. It is thus not surprising that the words "average" and "mean" designate both the middle way between unequal shares but also the accident, the disaster, that which is unfair or invidious.

∞ Insert: The question of a/symmetry in the rhizome

To further understand symmetry in communication, we will define symmetry as communication in which the communicative ability of the communicants is equal. Likewise, asymmetric communication is communication where there is a gap between the communicants that makes it impossible for them to enter into a relationship where they can freely communicate on an equal level. The notion of balance is able to bridge symmetric and asymmetric behaviour to a certain extent. As noted above, Watzlawick *et al.* observed how human interaction is either symmetric or complementary, based either on equality or difference.[258] In complementary interaction, one part assumes the role of the superior or primary communicant and the other that of the inferior or secondary communicant, such as in a mother-child or a teacher-pupil relationship.[259]

There can be various reasons for an asymmetrical communicative relationship. Among the most important are (from the point of view of the receiver) the power relationship, the request of a communication act, the interest in it, the ability to share communication channels with the sender of the message and the ability to interrupt the communication act. Asymmetrical communication

---

258 Ibid., 68–71.
259 Ibid.

in the rhizome is characterised by an attempt to gain power over the communication channels and by the fact that it is unable to handle conflict. It may produce conflict, but it always produces conflict for the other, never involving itself. When one node in the rhizome cuts off its incoming channels from another node and starts to communicate in a unidirectional way, the node which now only receives information but cannot directly send it, still has ways of getting back to the sender's node. It can choose a number of other channels bypassing other nodes, which however makes the procedure unproductive: more energy is spent on communicating back and there is a higher probability that the answer changes until it reaches the destination.

A practical example: among the most asymmetrical communication media today are billboards and unsolicited spam mail. They are not explicitly desired, they are often of no interest, one cannot communicate back using the same communication channels, and they cannot be interrupted. The gap in the power relationship arises from the economic power the sender enjoys over the receiver but the asymmetry in the power relationship already arises from the accumulated asymmetry of the other factors.

The "friendliest" type of asymmetric communication, because it is the most unconditional one, is that of sun rays. As McLuhan observed, electric light is the only medium without a message, which is true for any light in general—"unless it is used to spell out some verbal ad or name."[260] Thus, the sun is wholly disinterested and would exist without anyone being there to consume its energy. The sun gives freely and at all times. In McLuhan, Bataille's observation also resonates: "Solar energy is the source of life's exuberant development. The origin and essence of our wealth are given in the radiation of the sun, which dispenses energy—wealth—without

---

260   McLuhan, Understanding Media, 8. Sebeok however rightly observes that "luminance requires a living interpreter" (Sebeok, Global Semiotics, 17).

any return."[261] It must be noted though that McLuhan and Bataille eclipse an important point, namely that the sun has no choice but to disperse its energy. The sun is a prime example of productive asymmetric communication in that it is not interested, but this disinterestedness goes so far that it may be considered wholly unintentional and mechanistic.

---

261 Bataille, The Accursed Share, 28.

4 Economy: sharing the home

It is inevitable that topics like friendship/enmity and gift/
countergift, as well as those deriving from these pairs, lead to
the topic of hospitality. We have seen how some of these notions
fail to describe today's place of commercial communications. As
was mentioned in the previous chapter, the lack of love inherent
in a commercial communication act makes it nearly impossible
to describe these acts in Derrida's terms of friendship or the gift
even though they fulfil the conditions of non-recognition and
asymmetry; Bataille's general economy of exuberance seems to
better describe the advertising frenzy but makes it difficult to
model the countergift on advertising practiced as a one-way
discipline. The central problem with all these theories is that
they dodge the possibility of a refusal: refusal of friendship, of
enmity, of the gift or the countergift. They propose ideals of these
notions, ideals which in some way appear as something continuous: the only rupture—the final, impossible and everlasting rupture—being at the end of the relationship: death. The issue of
death is difficult to grasp in a daily economic context. It marks
the biological death of an entity, but as we have seen, commercial
entities do not underlie the same biological cycles as human beings. The Roman Catholic Church, for instance, is nearly 2000
years old;[262] the Hudson Bay Company over 330 years.

---

262 The Church continues to have one of the best-known audio logos.

We thus need to look for a concept that gives place for a rupture and accommodates our lifespan, while still keeping in mind our finality and our place in the great rhizome. This concept—proposed as a hypothesis—is that of hospitality. Hospitality bears within it the ideas of friendship/enmity and gift/countergift and is closely linked to the house, to the dwelling place. Dwelling, as Heidegger teaches us, essentially means to build, to be, and—most importantly—to think.[263] As such, dwelling is deeply rooted in life: "Dwelling itself is always a staying with things. Dwelling, as preserving, keeps the fourfold in that with which mortals stay: in things."[264] Though it may appear that dwelling is essentially a sedentary concept, it cannot be denied that nomads dwell too. Dwelling means living with things, with objects but also—if dwelling points to thinking—with texts, thoughts, ideas, worldviews. In short: Living with things is living in community. *Thing* means gathering,[265] which is still present in the Nordic languages (*stortinget* is the Norwegian parliament; *stor*=big). According to KLUGE, the German *Ding* is to be traced back to "that, which is debated on the thing",[266] that is, that which is debated in the gathering of the community. Neither KLUGE nor other sources make mention that the *ting,* the gathering, would have the double character of "agora" as the place where the debate *and* the market take place.

If dwelling points to living in community it follows that dwelling must deal with the diverse forces being present in and on the borders of a community, and that dwelling must thus become a question of sharing physical and mental space.

---

263 Heidegger, Basic Writings, 349. It is surprising that Heidegger in Building Dwelling Thinking does not mention the *Bauer,* the farmer, cultivator or protector.
264 Ibid., 353.
265 Ibid., 355.
266 KLUGE, "Ding".

4.1   Hospitality

To answer the question of economy, any economy, but a communication economy in particular, we must follow the question of hospitality. Economy does not initially refer to a commercial activity but to the herd, the house, the household. According to KLUGE, economy is derived from *oikos*, house, and *némein*, to share, divide, distribute *(teilen, verteilen)*. Economy is thus the question of sharing the house, the question of whom to admit and whom to expel. The type of permission it grants, if it grants it, is a permission that involves she who gives permission.[267] Admittance into one's home is not only a licence to do something, but to do it under the roof of the host, to do it together with and in the presence of the host. It is not a grant that can be given without involving the host but is intricately tied to her.

The question of hospitality is of importance for a number of reasons. First of all, it is, along with forgiving, mourning and giving one of the aporias that Derrida dedicates considerable thought to and we expect to find some of the same oppositional forces at work in hospitality. Second, the question of hospitality has become a major concern with the inroads of communication channels into our homes. This reading of hospitality can be taken literally to make out the fickle borders between what divides and unites the private and the public. The third reading of the question of hospitality is a metaphorical one and closely tied to the question of the brain and the mind. It opens the field of thinking the possibilities of offering hospitality in our minds. When the distinctions between the public and private blur or retreat altogether and hospitality in our homes can no longer be offered in the traditional

---

267   The *xenos*, the stranger, the guest, shall be grammatically treated as masculine and the host as feminine to make distinctions more easily available. I will however not use the term "hostess" because its many meanings imply a kind of servitude.

sense, then what we are left with is our mind. The questions to be asked are: what is allowed to cater to our minds? What do we willingly offer hospitality to and when can we make out a violation of hospitality such as an occupation against our wills diminishing our present and future ability to offer hospitality? The realm of hospitality is where Heidegger's observation that *ethos* means abode or dwelling place comes in.[268] When we talk about dwelling, we thus also talk about ethics.

Hospitality, if it is to be sustainable, must have one of the characteristics of a pure public good: non-diminishability; but traditional hospitality (as opposed to absolute hospitality which appears unsustainable) need not take into account the other characteristic, that of non-exclusion.[269] Derrida highlights the antagonistic forces between traditional and absolute hospitality:

> It is a question of knowing how to transform and improve the law, and of knowing if this improvement is possible within an historical space which takes place between the law of an unconditional hospitality, offered a priori to every other, to all newcomers, whoever they may be, and the conditional laws of a right to hospitality, without which the unconditional law of hospitality would be in danger of remaining a pious and irresponsible desire, without form and without potency, and of even being perverted at any moment.[270]

In brief, we can say that unconditional or absolute hospitality is the impossible kind of hospitality because its aim is to be open to all that comes and not reject anyone who wants or needs to be offered shelter. It is the sovereign's handing over of sovereignty, the dissolution of any sovereign space. Conditional or traditional

---

268   Heidegger, Basic Writings, 256.
269   For the definition of a public good, see Stiglitz, Economics of the Public Sector, 128.
270   Derrida, On Cosmopolitanism and Forgiveness, 22f.

hospitality on the other hand is a diffuse concept that is intuitively understood and practiced but without a clear understanding of the point of rupture.

The notion of non-diminishability takes us to the question of *teilen* as sharing versus dividing up in order to share. We recall what we said in the beginning of the chapter "Communication as being-with-others": when we share goods, we divide them, give away a part and the keep the rest. When we share thoughts, we give them away entirely and keep them in their entirety; when a thought is given away, it is multiplied and not transferred. Hospitality involves both goods, that is, physical entities of which there is only a certain amount at disposal, as well as thoughts and ideas. The signification of the physical part of sharing one's home is evident: the share of a physical space diminishes with every additional body that dwells in it. The non-material aspect however has two components: living with a foreigner, a new body or entity, there is inevitably an exchange, or rather interchange, of thoughts and ideas which were never before possible. The coming together of two bodies, two nodes in the rhizome, leads to a new constellation enabling generation, invention, qualitative growth (what we have previously called organic or energetic intelligence). The opposite: deadlock, inertia, even regression, may also take place in a situation of hospitality, and the most striking explanation for such a deadlock or a natural limit to hospitality is the diminishability of an enclosed physical space. The other enclosed space at stake, mental space, is physical on a microscopic level but it is no less real and no less threatened by an exuberant offering of hospitality. Constantly being around another body or around a piece of information bears the danger that this presence may come to occupy our minds to a degree that blocks out any possibility for generating. If we cannot withdraw to formulate our own thoughts (the act Nietzsche called for in the opening quote of this book), the foreigner's thoughts or what arises in the interchange of ideas will channel and limit the development of novel combinations in and of the world. If the mind cannot rest, it will eventually go insane. The difficulty is to know when the mind is being unduly occupied and—once this is recognised—to act accordingly. This may result in a rupture with hospitality but this rupture is necessary to offer hospitality in the long run.

4.1.1   The questions of the host and the foreigner

In *Of Hospitality*, Derrida opens his seminar on the Foreigner Question offering two readings of "the question of the foreigner":

> Isn't the question of the foreigner [*l'étranger*] a foreigner's question? Coming from the foreigner, from abroad [*l'étranger*]?
> Before saying *the* question of the foreigner, perhaps we should also specify: question *of* the foreigner.
> [...]
> [T]he question of the foreigner is a question *of* the foreigner, addressed *to* the foreigner. As though the foreigner were first of all *the one who* puts the first question or *the one to whom* you address the first question. [271]

The foreigner, the other who is strange or from abroad, that is: outlandish, asks permission to be let in. This question inaugurates a cycle of questions or rather: it is the first question which is not the first question since the question has already triggered a counterquestion prior to its posing. We may try to understand this in situational terms. Let us imagine a stranger, a foreigner, a weirdo, an outcast, who asks to be let in, who seeks shelter. Even

---

271   Derrida, Of Hospitality, 3.

before the *xenos* is able to formulate his question, he knocks on the door of our home. Prior to knocking, he has not existed in our lives, so the questions the knock triggers are "why this knock? who is at the door? who asks for entrance?" These questions arise the moment the stranger's knuckles touch the door. Though the stranger's intention precedes the knock, the question of the host, that is, the question posed by the potential host, posed perhaps only in the host's mind, and perhaps not even knowingly, evolves simultaneously as the knock. Is the knock preceding the question of the host? Is it not the host's door, her house, her dwelling place, that ultimately asks the stranger to enter? The home anticipates the stranger's request, which in turn exists in virtuality before any object comes into view which might answer his request. The question is actualised, targeted, when a home which might offer shelter turns up. It is actualised when there is something to which a question can be asked. But is the question in virtuality not always there? If to dwell means to erect a building, is not the building already the answer to an unasked question, to the question *of* the foreigner? Is the building not a question mark ("do you need shelter?")? Flusser observes how today's buildings have become dysfunctional and proposes that houses be built so that they attract interpersonal relationships: "Such an attractive house would have to collect relationships, process them into information, store and relay them. A creative [schöpferisch] house as node of the interhuman web."[272]

The building establishes immediately a certain boundary between the public and the private, between outside and inside. It establishes a rupture, a change in sovereign territory, which is the prerequisite for hospitality. The building itself stands for the possibility of hospitality and thus not only answers an unasked question but inaugurates a discourse, a ping-pong of questions, requests,

272 Flusser, *Medienkultur*, 162.

desires, urges, answers and needs. *The home produces the stranger.* It poses the question of intimacy, where the intimate is not only the innermost, the familiar, the familial, but also its opposite, the *inimicus*, the (private) enemy: "The brother or the enemy, the brother enemy, is the question, the questioning form of the question, this question that I ask because it is first of all put to me."[273] *Freund/ Feind, amicus/inimicus, hospes/hostis,* hospitality/hostility: these oppositions show the close link between friend and fiend to such an extent that they cannot be separated. These antagonistic forces, if we are to term them such, come together in the notion of "hostire", the Latin word for equalize, compensate, requite or recompense.

In his 1959 short story *Mortality and Mercy in Vienna*, Thomas Pynchon not only reminds us of the reading of host as a receiver of guests and as an enemy. Lupescu, the protagonist's apparent Doppelgänger, hands him over his apartment just before a party is to take place: "You are now the host. As host you are a trinity: (a) receiver of guests [...] (b) an enemy and (c) an outward manifestation, for them, of the divine body and blood."[274] Thus, host can also refer to the altar bread, the Corpus Christi: "And [Jesus] took bread, gave thanks and broke it, and gave it to them, saying, 'This is my body given for you; do this in remembrance of me.'"[275] In the communion, in the act of sharing, the host (Jesus) gives his guests (the communicants) a manifestation of himself before the perishing of his irreplaceable, singular body. "This is my body given *for* you": Jesus compensates his body that will no longer be with a representation or a symbol of it, but he also compensates or equalizes the sins of others by giving his very life. To accept that the host (the bread) *is* in fact the body of Christ as the Catholic Church does, and not just its representation, requires a leap of faith. This

---

273   Derrida, The Politics of Friendship, 150.
274   Pynchon, Mortality and Mercy in Vienna.
275   Luke 22:19.

leap of faith has the same quality as the one that must be taken at the threshold to the house, that is, at the limit of hospitality.

What is the question the home asks by virtue of being a home? It does not ask the question "are you inside or outside?" because it already establishes the answer to that question. The home is the object that signifies the inside/outside distinction in the first place. The first question the home asks is "are you a friend or an enemy?" but this question is already futile since it does not expect an answer. It cannot accept an honest answer since it is posed prior to the contact between the potential host and the potential guest, prior to establishing a relationship. Yet this is the crucial question, the unanswerable, impossible question: impossible for its seemingly clear-cut distinction between friend and enemy but also impossible for its untimeliness. It is a question that tries to bring the future to the present. It questions the *intention* of he who is outside but at a point where these intentions are purely virtual because the stranger does not yet know the host. The stranger may regard the host as much as a threat as the host regards the stranger. Since the question knows very well of this impossibility, as well as the unlikeliness that someone would announce himself as an enemy, it remains on hold, it hovers over the house.[276] It remains there, the patron saint of the home, the question which envelops the home in such a way that the foreigner is always put in question for the time of his stay, "as though the foreigner were being-in-question, the very question of being-in-question, the question-being or the being-in-question of the question. But also the one who, putting the first question, puts me in question."[277] Derrida puts this question at the beginning of a relationship between the foreigner and the host but the question does not vanish

276 We must remark here, however, that it does occur that someone announ-
   ces himself as an enemy intruder. In *Of Hospitality* Derrida mentions two
   Biblical stories that will be exemplified below.
277 Derrida, Of Hospitality, 3.

once the host has decided that the foreigner would be worthy of the gift of hospitality.

4.1.2   The rules of the sovereign

What question would the host ask, once she perceives the knock on the door, opens it and beholds the foreigner, the question, before her eyes? What is the real, manifested question beyond those ruminations on questions as such? What is the content of the question? "This foreigner, then, is someone with whom, to receive him, you begin by asking his name; you enjoin him to state and guarantee his identity, as you would a witness before a court."[278] Back to the court, symbolised by the balance and the sword, the play between balance and decision, between the weight and counterweight of life and the putting to death. "You begin by asking his name": Pure hospitality cannot allow itself to ask a name, to inquire about an identity. And even without the context of pure, unconditional hospitality we do not even begin by asking the foreigner. We begin by asking *ourselves*, and we do not ask ourselves the name of the foreigner but his intentions. This will likely lead to the question of identity, of a name and an origin (this is the rigid, governmental identity, not the constantly evolving biological identity[279]), but it is not what is at the beginning of meeting a foreigner.[280] We do not

---

278   Ibid., 27.
279   Badiou does not work with this governmental type of identity but with a qualitative one: "An identity is a number of traits by which an individual or a group recognises itself as 'it self'. [The self] is that which, through all characteristic traits of identity, remains more or less invariant in its infinite web of differences and changes." Badiou, Wofür steht der Name Sarkozy? 69.
280   There is a significant difference in the way different cultures answer the telephone. In Switzerland, one mostly says one's name first so that the caller can identify if the right person is on the phone. In Anglo-Saxon countries, the typical phrase upon answering the phone is "hello?" which asks for the caller's name. Call display is putting an end to this necessity since it enables us to see whose telephone is calling before answering the phone—which

so much want to know who it is as what he wants—and we know we will never find out because the question of intention is fluid (as is, but to a lesser degree, identity) while the name is rigid. The host first weighs the intentions of the foreigner versus hers before she weighs the identity of the foreigner versus hers. The identity of the foreigner, if he tells the truth, is fixed in the past and will likely only slowly evolve. At the same time, the foreigner already embodies an answer to that question: his name is "Stranger" and his origin is "Elsewhere", or more precisely: "Outside". The intention may all of a sudden change as it is confronted with more information. The question of the name and origin is only asked once while the question of intention is asked time and again—not openly but in the host's and the stranger's mind. Identity is asked and intention is questioned.

But who is that host who dares ask the question of identity and, over and over, the question of intention? Who is she to bring the foreigner to court? The host is the *petty sovereign* over home and herd, bed and bath, air and space within certain narrow limits. As a *grand petty sovereign*, which is often a he, she is also master[281] over those who live under her roof. The sovereign of the house is she who makes the rules of the house and decides when the rules are suspended. "The paradox of sovereignty is expressed as follows: 'the sovereign is at the same time inside and outside the legal order,'" Agamben writes.[282] The sovereign of the house is indeed included in the legal order, but this legal order can only be guaranteed by that which is able to suspend it,[283] by that which

---

may further lead to refusing a call only because no number or an unknown number shows uFurthermore, call display can be misleading since it only displays the name or number to whom the telephone is registered.

281   Again, like hostess, mistress has a set of connotations that should be avoided.

282   Agamben, Homo Sacer, 25.

283   Ibid., 27.

is outside the legal order or rather, that which is able to elevate itself above the legal order at will. Following Agamben, we can say that the sovereign's basic lawmaking and lawbreaking power is the proclamation of the state of exception, the suspension of the rules. The sovereign decides whether the normal state of affairs is in effect taking place.[284] Derrida, on the other hand, would say that the sovereign is marked by her ability to forgive the unforgivable, an act Schirmacher deconstructs by claiming that one can only forgive oneself.[285] If Schirmacher is right, what follows is that the sovereign is only sovereign over herself. We shall nevertheless follow the other trajectories and work with the idea of sovereignty, because no matter how inexistent or deconstructed the sovereign is, there is still embedded in us, as in many animals, a sense of property, a desire for a "home to want to come home to",[286] and even Schirmacher would claim the right to expel something or someone from the space he considers his own.

The suspension of rules is only applicable to the sovereign's territory and not an inch beyond. In the concrete case of the house, the sovereign's territory is smaller than the sovereign's property. The sovereign of the home is only sovereign (with exceptions that shall be treated in a moment) within the walls of the house—where the gaze of the state cannot penetrate. The state sovereign's blindness produces the sovereignty of the home. The home is the blind spot *(der tote Winkel)* of the state. It is an area the state does not control because it does not have the resources to do so or it believes that the home shall be the place reserved for transgressions so that the people are docile outside of it. Derrida's claims that "the State cannot guarantee or claim to guarantee the private domain (for it is a domain), other than by controlling it and trying to penetrate

---

284   Agamben, Homo Sacer, 25.
285   Derrida, Seminar on Forgiveness at the European Graduate School Paris satellite, April 2004.
286   Diprose, Responsibility in a Place and Time of Terror, §7.

it to be sure of it."[287] We should word this paradox differently: the state can only guarantee the private domain by not controlling it. However, it can only be sure of it by penetrating it. Schirmacher claims that there is no sovereign territory in the first place, that territory itself is a defunct notion.[288] There is some truth to this, and one indication of it is the fusion and confusion of notions of the private and the public. Territory can be read in a literal sense where it refers to *terra*, ground, property, and this reading indicates how difficult it is to draw the lines between inside and outside. The other reading of sovereign territory is that of an opening, it is the space for freedom, the opposing force to determination, and denying or disregarding this reading, albeit metaphorical, would amount to a denial of the opening of freedom.

There have been regimes and times, and there still are, where homes have been tapped on a regular basis: an enormous squandering of energy for a gigantic pile of information that produced more enemies of the state than many wars. With the Internet, the situation has somewhat changed, and there has been a shift of surveillance from the seemingly private to the seemingly public domain. This distinction of domains can of course not be upheld for very long since the Internet is a network operating with one protocol designed for public, private and work use. Consequently, what is to be found about a person on the Internet is often a mixture of his or her public, private and work engagements. We, and others with or without our knowledge or permission, 'happily' and actively work at the deprivatisation of our lives, as Anders might say.[289] We are happily poking holes into the walls of our home and we are willingly paying for this, as Anders noted in his pessimistic critique of TV and radio: "Each consumer is an unpaid

287 Derrida, Of Hospitality, 55.
288 Schirmacher, personal communication, 6 June 2007.
289 Anders, Die Antiquiertheit des Menschen, Band II, 233.

homeworker for the production of the mass 'man'."[290] What does it mean if the state leaves homes untouched, untapped, to leave room for transgression? First of all, it means that the state leaves this space open in order to have docile bodies, bodies that follow the rules of the community outside the house. It gives space for an everyday carnival to squander surplus energy. Even though the home is not an entirely extralegal territory since it always is on the territory of a nation state, it is an enclave to the state *where the gaze of the state or that of passers-by cannot penetrate*. (This means that the front yard is not extralegal territory. It also means that the house is not extralegal territory when the gaze can penetrate it: one is not allowed to have an orgy with the blinds up.) If this is self-understood, it may lead to believing that the private is but the pretence for the concealment of forbidden activities. In any case, by giving the home an extralegal status of sorts, the nation state, which produced the first foreigner when drawing the lines of its territory, produces another foreigner, a private foreigner.

4.1.3   The threshold

If the setting and suspending of the rules of the house is the petty sovereign's task, her contribution to a legal order of the *confined territory of the house*, and if this decides on who is expelled, exiled, who loses the rights of hospitality, of the community, who—as bare life—may be killed but not sacrificed,[291] then there is a more basic function the host fulfils which precedes this suspension of rules: that of the gatekeeper, the concierge, the watchdog:

> I want to be master at home, to be able to receive whomever I like there. Anyone who encroaches on my 'at home' [...] on my power of

---

290   Anders, Die Antiquiertheit des Menschen, Band I, 101.
291   Agamben, Homo Sacer, 18.

hospitality, on my sovereignty as host, I start to regard as an undesirable foreigner, and virtually as an enemy.[292]

Before the foreigner enters the house, he is outside the petty sovereign's territory; hence she has no sovereign powers over the foreigner. Only by the grace of the host, which may just as well be calculation, is the foreigner included in the community of the house, is he liberated from the laws of the outside and confined by those of the inside. *The inclusion precedes the exclusion while denial of access precedes and precludes the inclusion.* The sovereign cannot proclaim the state of exception over someone who is not tied to the sovereign and her territory. She cannot strip the political life off someone who is outside that political sphere, but, for whatever reasons, and there may be plenty, she can, if she follows the rules of traditional hospitality, deny access to her territory in the first place. As Arendt observes, the first deprivation of the rightless was that of their homes, that is, "their distinct place in the world", which was followed by the impossibility of finding a new home.[293] The rightless may be killed but not sacrificed. "The prolongation of their lives is due to charity and not to right, for no law exists which could force the nations to feed them; their freedom of movement, if they have it at all, gives them no right to residence which even the jailed criminal enjoys as a matter of course; and their freedom of opinion is a fool's freedom, for nothing they think matters anyhow."[294]

As we have seen, this invitation or denial of entry takes place at an undue time: at the threshold when the potential guest and the potential host behold each other for the first time—when they are neither inside nor outside but in a doubly extraterritorial space.

---

292 Derrida, Of Hospitality, 53f.
293 Arendt, The Portable Hannah Arendt, 34.
294 Ibid., 37.

This extraterritorial space, which may be likened to those at airports,[295] is the space for the contestation of knowledge about the foreigner and—in a reversed sense—the host. We want to know but we cannot. We want to know the intentions of the foreigner at a time when there is no information on either side of the threshold which would allow for drawing a reasonable conclusion as to the intentions. Of course, the foreigner has a specific request for otherwise he would not knock at the door but this request is based only on the one outside. To speak in terms of the scale: at the moment when it is decided whether to allow or deny access to the stranger, both the sovereign's and the foreigner's weight are put on a scale and compared to the other, but this balance or inequality is not yet contested, measured against, weighed up, spurred on.

The impossibility to decide whether to grant access or deny it is what must have led to the idea of absolute or pure hospitality, itself an impossible request. Derrida writes:

> [A]bsolute hospitality requires that I open up my home and that I give not only to the foreigner [...] but to absolute, unknown anonymous other, and that I give place to them, that I let them come, that I let them arrive, and take place in the place I offer them, without asking of them either reciprocity (entering into a pact) or even their names. The law of absolute hospitality commands a break with hospitality by right, with law or justice as rights.[296]

---

295 The extraterritorial space behind airport security checkpoints is a hyperbole of the threshold of the house. Sherrin Frances, who held a job as an airport security officer, writes in the introduction to her dissertation: "the passenger must provide any supplementary or background information asked of him, potentially putting his very identity on display. The shadows must be eradicated via spotlights and any barriers must be cleared of obstructions." Frances, Becoming Secure, 6.

296 Derrida, Of Hospitality, 25.

Absolute hospitality is the ethical response to the undecidability on the threshold to the house. It resolves the problem by not asking the question. Who are we to decide whether the foreigner needs our shelter? When we lack knowledge because we are not omniscient, a knowledge that greatly exceeds anything we might be able to find out about the foreigner over our preferred channels of information while he waits on the doorstep, how can we possibly decide the fate of the foreigner? How can we possibly come to a decision about the fate of the foreigner knocking at our door, if he is not within the confines of our sovereign territory? Absolute hospitality, in any case the first step of this absolute hospitality, requires, and this is not so much ethical as logical, that he enter our territory before we can decide on his expulsion. To be excluded, he must first be included.

Derrida brings up the story of Lot's challenge of hospitality[297] and sheds light on the limits of absolute hospitality. Lot offered hospitality to two foreigners (who happen to be angels). In the night, his house is all of a sudden surrounded by townspeople who ask him to turn over the foreigners so that they might abuse them.[298] For inconceivable reasons, Lot denies this request but, as a trade-off, offers his two daughters to the townspeople (who, in turn, refuse them). The guests drag Lot into the house before the outraged mob has a chance to violate him, and God strikes the door with blindness. The next morning, Lot and his lot can flee the town before it is destroyed. A nearly identical story if not more atrocious is recounted in Judges 19:15–30. There, the host offers his

297   Ibid., 153.
298   "abuse": This is the translation Derrida gives (153), that of the *Jerusalem Bible*; *Die Heilige Schrift* (translation: F. E. Schlachter, 1985) uses "erkennen", recognise, but in an ancient sense also fuck; the *Zwingli Bibel* uses "beiwohnen", assist, join, ancient for lie with; the *Bibel in heutigem Deutsch*, issued by the Deutsche Bibelgesellschaft, uses "Verkehr haben", to have intercourse. Genesis 19:1–9.

daughter to the crowd of townspeople who demand intercourse with the guest. The crowd refuses whereupon the guest gives them his concubine instead. They rape her and he finds her dead on the doorstep the next morning.[299]

These stories illustrate the limits of absolute hospitality and they end Derrida's fifth seminar, *Pas d'hospitalité*. In fact, Derrida asks us at the end: "Are we the heirs to this tradition of hospitality? Up to what point?"[300]

It must be conceded that these two stories, though carrying us to the extremes, are corrupted. Absolute hospitality requires an unconditional attitude, an unconditional offering of hospitality to the anonymous or unknown. Neither Lot nor the host of the Levite in Judges is faced with a situation that can be called entirely free of conditions. Neither proves to be a sovereign deserving this name. A true sovereign would not give son, daughter, wife or concubine *on the condition* that the guests remain intact, untouched. The sovereigns in these stories would have had two choices: to let the townspeople into the house and thus bind them by the rules of the house, which would enable to expel or kill them if they did not behave accordingly, or to shut the door, bar the windows and let no one inside, and if someone gained access by force, to kill him.[301] In these stories, the house was clearly not overcrowded when the townspeople tried to gain access to the foreigners. It was not yet facing the issue of the physical limitations of the dwelling place. Had the host expelled an inhabitant of the house to be able to receive another guest, prior to the townspeople's demand, the story would have been less outrageous. The second story, the

---

299   Derrida, Of Hospitality, 155.
300   Ibid., 155.
301   This brings to mind two of The Eleven Satanic Rules of the Earth by A.S. LaVey: "3. When in another's lair, show him respect or else do not go there. 4. If a guest in your lair annoys you, treat him cruelly and without mercy." http://www.churchofsatan.com/Pages/Eleven.html.

one reported in Judges, has another flaw that makes it difficult for us to consider the story a valid example of absolute hospitality: even though it was the sovereign who offered his daughter (which the townspeople refused to accept), it was in the end the guest who sacrificed, or rather, ditched, his concubine to literally save his own ass. The guest had to leave a part of himself, that is, his concubine, behind to be granted the kind of hospitality the host had in mind.

Another question that deserves some thought, though we are unlikely to draw a conclusion yet, is the following: if absolute hospitality, in Derrida's words, requires us to be open to the foreigner as such, to the unknown anonymous other,[302] and if this absolute hospitality is designed to resolve the undecidability of the threshold, what if these two conditions are not given? What if we are faced with a situation where those who demand, ask, beg for access to the house are known to the sovereign and, on top, their intentions are known? Do we offer absolute hospitality if we offer a friend shelter, even if this offer in no way is part of a pact or requires reciprocity? Can we be said to deny absolute hospitality when we do not let those in we know will disturb the peace of the home or question our sovereignty? Can it justly be called hospitality when we offer our home to someone and at the same time bind him by our rules, including the expulsion and the suspension of the rules? These decisions must be taken, and they can only be taken as impossible decisions, taken in an instant of madness.[303]

The decision haunts us because it defies the idea that the decision is a solution and that knowledge is required to make a decision. The process of coming to a decision may be called if not a solution then at least the ethical answer to the impossibility of the decision itself. The moment a decision is made, it cannot be called

---

302 Derrida, Of Hospitality, 25.
303 Derrida, The Gift of Death, 65.

ethical because it excludes everything it did not decide in favour of as well as everything that was not even in question.

> The knight of faith must not hesitate. He accepts his responsibility by heading off towards the absolute request of the other, beyond knowledge. He decides, but his absolute decision is neither guided nor controlled by knowledge. Such, in fact is the paradoxical condition of every decision: it cannot be deduced from a form of knowledge of which it would simply be the effect, conclusion, or explication.[304]

The decision thus requires a leap of faith. The decision about the foreigner must be made without prior knowledge because such knowledge is not available and if it were, would be only partial. The sovereign, however, cannot let herself be paralysed by the fundamental undecidability but must take this madness of decision as an urgent task. While it is true that we shape the biological and spiritual future in every moment of our lives, a skill Schirmacher attributes to homo generator,[305] it is evident that we cannot anticipate the future and must therefore assume responsibility based on a lack of knowledge.

4.1.4   Filtering

Before going to the extremes of hospitality and overriding previous notions of the role of the sovereign in her home, Derrida reminds us that "sovereignty can only be exercised by filtering, choosing, and thus by excluding and doing violence. Injustice [...] begins right away, from the very threshold of the right of

---

304   Ibid., 77.
305   Schirmacher: Homo Generator: Media and Postmodern Technology.

hospitality."[306] This violence is however not limited to filtering and exclusion. Elsewhere he claims that "being at home with oneself [...] supposes a reception or inclusion of the other which one seeks to appropriate, control, and master according to different modalities of violence [...]"[307] In other words, the inclusion risks neutralising what is included.[308] It is difficult to say which sovereign is stronger: she who offers absolute hospitality, who opens the door to the anonymous other, but may also be the one who cannot say "no", who is incapable of doing violence, even for self-protection; or she who exercises violence at the threshold by choosing and filtering, but may only do so because she fears the anonymous other.

Filtering is a poor measure to protect one's home, and this is due to this violence of exclusion before knowing what is excluded. It is an action that resides in passivity, especially if the faculty of filtering is relegated to something or someone else and because the act of filtering stops any kind of contact from which a bilateral relationship might evolve. Filtering is that which appears to enable us to tell friend from foe but it does it in an imperfect way. It is the mode of adapting to technology, of saving sovereignty, exercised by she who is, if not in control then at least holder or addressee of the communication channels. Filtering is the kind of technological adaptation or flexibility that can only grow from resignation with uneven power or communication structures. It is a way of getting adapted to technology, instead of generating technology. If the power structure is fundamentally unequal, sometimes there can only be resignation, but resignation and filtering are unproductive in a fatal sense. They take power relations for granted and absorb them. They deprive the relationship, unequal as it may be, of any kind of feedback, of any

306 Derrida, Of Hospitality, 55.
307 Derrida, On Cosmopolitanism and Forgiveness, 16f.
308 Derrida, The Politics of Friendship, viii.

effort to render it more symmetrical. Who engages in filtering may save time and nerves but he or she becomes automatically complicit with the unbalanced, asymmetrical power structures.

Filtering, and it is helpful to think of filtering in terms of to-day's email spam filters[309], cannot be flawless. Filter, according to KLUGE, derives from Mid-Latin *filtrum*, a sieve made of felt.[310] The nineteenth century German word *filzen*, to search someone, initially meant to comb.[311] Thus, filtering is not only a sieve with holes of a certain size that retain the elements that are bigger than the holes and let the others pass (there are filtering mechanisms that keep what is too large for the mesh and others that keep what comes out at the bottom). Filtering is an activity that searches for certain indications to categorise that which is filtered. The categor-ies and indications according to which we categorise are based on experience and rely on the assumption that what we encounter is something which follows the patterns of our experience. Hence there is a certain possibility that we filter out that which we would like to keep only because it follows patterns that we usually ex-clude, and we will not even know about it since we have excluded it in the first place. Not only do we not know what we erroneously have filtered out: that which is filtered out, if it is not an actor but rather a representation of an actor, such as a spam email, will not know about it either. If a communication situation is technically designed for a one-way information transfer, the sender, that is, the potential guest will not know that he is being excluded and may continue to address us.

We may distinguish active and passive filters. Active filters are those the sovereign herself employs when faced with a foreigner, and passive filters are those the sovereign lets someone or something

---

309   Filters need not only be technological ones: perception, interest, resources, time, etc. are the filters we use every day.

310   KLUGE, "Filter".

311   Ibid., "filzen".

else employ. The active filter may offer better matches because she who is faced with the prospect of sharing something with the foreigner decides for herself—using filters which are dependent on the momentary state of mind—who is admitted, but the activity of filtering may at times consume so many resources that the sovereign is not left with any to dedicate to hospitality. When we leave the dirty work of deciding who is an undesired, unfriendly other to the passive filter, we can stay at home and offer hospitality to the other. This hospitality is however not entirely satisfactory because we never know if someone else is at the door ringing the bell we have turned off, someone who is in greater need of our shelter or someone who is more appreciative or offers a greater probability for the generation of something new.

If the sovereign wants to hold her fortress, she has to leave it, she has to endanger herself and actively engage in the battle on the open field. Not only does she lose her sovereign territory when she is defeated. She can also not offer hospitality while she is not "at home". If the sovereign builds stronger walls, she may not immediately be defeated, but neither is the intruder. To speak in terms of unsolicited spam mail: if we have more powerful filters, the spammer will continue to spam us (potentially dodging our filter), although it may not end up in our mailbox, and at the same time, mails from loved ones are scanned and potentially sorted out before we get them. The spammer never receives a feedback whether his email went into the void or is undesired, so he continues—a machinery of unproductivity.[312]

---

312 The Swiss Confederation estimates that 80–90% of email traffic is spam. "Informationssicherung: Lage in der Schweiz und international – Halbjahresbericht 2006/II", 6. www.melani.admin.ch.

4.2   Architectures of the home

We think of the home as a space that is separated from the out-side and closed against an intrusion by the outside.[313] However, this "Biedermeier concept of the 'home'" is no longer valid since the home is the space which opens us the door to the outside and allows us to make contact with it.[314] At the same time, the mentality of being at home is carried to the outside world: we behave in public as we would do at home, Anders claims—even before the proliferation of cell phones and laptops.[315] Eric McLuhan claimed in a television broadcast that "there was no privacy in American homes. If you wanted privacy, you went out. Now this is changing. You don't go to the theatre anymore for privacy because there is advertising there now."[316] Though he points to something which bears truth, namely that the confusion of the public and private, but most of all consumer and citizen enforced by the advertising complex, has reached the home, his argument is not exactly valid anymore. We cannot remain at home if we want to avoid advertising. In fact, there is advertising at home, at work, in pub-lic, in private and the distinction of the borders becomes more complex if not futile. Derrida calls for a better understanding of these borders:

> Nowadays, a reflection on hospitality presupposes, among other things, the possibility of a rigorous delimitation of thresholds or frontiers: between the familial and the non-familial, between the

---

313   Anders, Die Antiquiertheit des Menschen, Band II, 83.
314   Ibid., 84.
315   Ibid., 85. Cell phones and laptops not only have the peculiarity that they carry the domestic behaviour to the public; they also carry the work behaviour to the private and public and the private to work.
316   "Marshall McLuhan's ABC", TV Ontario, 3 Dec. 2002, 21h.

foreign and the non-foreign, the citizen and the non-citizen, but first of all between the private and the public, private and public law, etc.[317]

Before questioning and broadening the concept of the sovereign, we shall look at different architectures of the home; mental constructs which each in its own way deals with the delimitation of the home and the environment: the castle, the windowless nomad and the home without walls. Each can be read as a metaphor for one's mind and the mindset one adapts in relation to one's environment.

∞ Insert: Two observations on the home

We have not considered the home in detail and there are a number of proposals and observations that do not fit in the linear structure of this book but should still be borne in mind.

Buildings are per sé beautiful because they are the place of dwelling. The killer argument in any discussion about art or advertising on public grounds is that of ugly architecture. What leads up to this argument is a shift from objective to aesthetic notions. As Gossage observed, "the row then becomes a matter of comparative beauty and one can go on haggling about that forever."[318] The aesthetic line of argument is also misleading due to its irrelevancy: "what a billboard looks like has nothing to do with whether it ought to be there."[319] As was mentioned before, street advocates of billboard advertising often claim that billboards are not really the issue with so many ugly buildings and ugly art all over—an argument the advertising industry would not dare to advance because it touches

---

317 Derrida, Of Hospitality, 47f.
318 Gossage, The Book of Gossage, 112.
319 Ibid., 113.

sensitive territory. When we claim that buildings are *per sé* beautiful then we are not talking about the same kind of aesthetics that people have in mind when comparing the beauty of billboards and buildings, of art and advertising: the beauty of buildings is to be seen in functional contrast to billboards or art, which have no material function but merely a mental one. The world is *per sé* beautiful because it is the place of dwelling. So is the house. Buildings that are designed for killing—perhaps this is as moralistic as it sounds—are conversely horrific and ugly structures. We believe inhabitants of "ugly" buildings to be "ugly" people. "Ugly" is to be understood as "displeasing" and does not refer to a specific feature such as "run-down". We believe that inhabitants of mansions resemble them in some way, in clothing or lifestyle. Design buildings are inhabitet by people in design clothing, middle-class buildings are inhabited by people wearing middle-class clothing.

It is illegal not to have a shelter.
Anyone who has been woken up by a police officer in a local park or even in the open field knows that it is illegal to sleep outside at night (paradoxically, it is not illegal to sleep outside in the daytime). Every nation state has different laws for sleeping on public grounds. Norway is one of the few countries that allows for camping on public property if certain conditions are fulfilled. In most other countries it is illegal. The sanctioning of a breach of this law indicates that *it is illegal not to have a home*. The reason for this is no doubt based on the state's accessibility to its citizens and visitors.[320] Without a home address, there is no place to deposit the

---

320 Nebraska state senator Ernie Chambers sued God for threatening him and the people of Nebraska and inflicting "widespread death, destruction and terrorisation of millions upon millions of the Earth's inhabitants". The case was thrown out because the defendant had no address and legal papers could not be served. The plaintiff in turn replied that the court had acknowledged the existence of God and thus recognised God's omniscience. "Since

papers, no place to collect taxes, no place for the official encounter of the state and the private person. If, as we will propose later on, the notion of the home is replaced by the notion of the mind, the same holds true. Those who "are not in their right mind" are not exactly illegal but they are stripped of their responsibility and their sovereignty—like the homeless, the vagabonds, the vagrants, gypsies and nomads who carry their home with them wherever they go: all those who have their home return to them whenever they need it and not vice versa. They are denied the status of full citizens because the state is unable to meet them on the implicit place of encounter: the private home or the right mind.

4.2.2   The castle

My home is my castle. It is my castle with the entire violence of the term.[321] The privileged spot where the castle is erect offers a panoptic view of the surroundings. Its walls,[322] its moat, its towers, its arrow slits, the tectonics of its geography are designed or chosen in such a way that the inhabitants of the castle remain secure under an attack. The castle is monumental, commanding, exalted. Its friendly gaze is gentle, protective, centralised. Its unfriendly gaze is imposing and threatening. It offers the safety of a legal system and a sovereign who is both inside and outside this legal system.

God knows everything [...] God has notice of this lawsuit." BBC, Legal case against God dismissed.

321   We refer to castle as the German "Burg", fortress, and not so much to the "Schloss", the palace-castle. Both were built for dwelling but the palace-castle had more representative functions than the fortress, which was primarily built for defence. For a brief history of the functional development of castles/fortresses, see De Landa, War in the Age of Intelligent Machines, 49ff.

322   Flusser reminds us that the *Mauer* (wall) has the same root as *munire*, to protect oneself (Flusser, Medienkultur, 161). KLUGE does not make this connection but, like Flusser, also points to the relationship between *murus* and munition.

The castle shares many features of the medieval city confined within walls. The castle has a twin function: to offer protection and to destroy the enemy who is challenging the sovereign territory. The walls and the moat offer protection; the arrow slits and the panoptic view secure an advantage over the unfriendly intruder. In order to perform this double function, arms both for defence and offence are employed though defence (self-protection) and offence (destruction of the enemy) are intertwined, and the protection of the sovereign and her people often means the destruction, or at least, putting to flight of the enemy.

The castle is also a deadly trap as countless tragedies can testify. The castle under siege is a prison cut off from its surroundings and from commerce by the same walls and moat designed for the protection of its inhabitants. The castle as such is a defensive structure: a powerful but inert construction. The thicker the walls, the heavier the weaponry of the intruder, which in turn triggers again a thickening of the walls: "The evolution of defense technology has been mostly driven by refinements in artillery and, vice versa, better defenses have often stimulated development in offensive techniques."[323] To meet the threat of a siege, the castle performs a further function, that of storage of provisions and weapons.

Under certain circumstances, the sovereign has to leave her home if she wants to maintain her long-term ability to offer hospitality. By leaving the home she endangers herself in the open field and—when she is defeated—loses her ability to offer hospitality. Not only may she lose her sovereign territory when defeated; she can also not offer hospitality while she is not at home.

Hospitality is offered within the confines of the castle and formidable machinery is at work to protect and maintain its ability to offer hospitality. This hospitality can however not be termed absolute as the very structure of the castle is a desperate attempt to stay alive

---

323   De Landa, War in the Age of Intelligent Machines, 48.

and not let the ultimate gift, the gift of death take place. It is an architecture of power that tries to evade the issue of the absolute outside world by establishing an absolute, sovereign inner world. In terms of structural defence it is a hyperbole of today's houses yet toned down in its ability to communicate with the outside. The issue of balance between safety and openness has been decided in favour of safety. Therefore, the castle is built so that it is a central node of communication where all outside channels are bundled and controlled.

4.2.3   The home without walls

Several scholars[324] make mention of the various forms of our porous homes. They observe how our dwelling place has opened up to the outside world by means of doors and windows as well as data connections, such as one-way (radio, television) and two-way-media (telephone, fax, e-mail). As mentioned in the first chapter, this is an indication of the confusion between public and private, and Derrida claims that this "renders impossible the hospitality, the right to hospitality, which it ought to make possible."[325]

The institution or the concept or the law of hospitality is what enables us to welcome someone; it enables us to tell guest from parasite. Without hospitality, any new arrival will be received as a parasite, "a guest who is wrong, illegitimate, clandestine, liable to expulsion or arrest."[326] It appears indeed evident that these holes in the walls of our homes, especially teletopes such as the telephone, impede if not our right or duty to offer hospitality, then certainly the quality of it. How can one give hospitality that deserves this name and engage in an intimate relationship with the guest, when Jehova's witnesses keep knocking at the door and telemarketers are

---

324 Anders, Die Antiquiertheit des Menschen, Band II; Derrida, Of Hospitality;
        Flusser, Medienkultur.
325 Derrida, Of Hospitality, 65.
326 Ibid., 61.

calling our homes, when the cell phone is ringing and our inbox beeping? The electronic media have the advantage that they may be turned off at anytime but this does not only turn off the channels of the parasite but also the channels of hospitality. "The current technological developments are restructuring space in such a way that what constitutes a space of controlled and circumscribed property is just what opens it to intrusion."[327] Derrida does not propose a way to resolve this problem but appears concerned with what this porosity means for the concept of hospitality.

> The safe house with roof, wall, window and door now only exists in fairytales. Material and immaterial wires have perforated it like an Emmentaler cheese: on the roof the antenna, through the wall the telephone wire, television instead of windows, and a garage with car instead of the door. The holy house became a ruin with cracks through which the wind of communication blows. This is shabby patchwork. A new architecture is needed.[328]

Flusser takes a different path. In a short essay entitled "Häuser bauen",[329] building houses, he writes that windows and doors have become dysfunctional, not only for the reasons just mentioned but also for the very fact that they may exclude us, the sovereign, as much as they may exclude the foreigner.[330] He locates the roof as that which divides the sovereign territory (i.e. the law of the state)

---

327   Ibid.
328   Flusser, Medienkultur, 162.
329   Ibid., 160–163. Since it is such a brief essay, this paragraph will not refer every one of Flusser's statements to a page number.
330   In a seminar with Žižek in Saas-Fee in August 2006, he pointed to another indication that walls have become dysfunctional (he repeated a similar statement in an interview I held with him in August 2006 which is available at www.youtube.com): "There is an institute within the Israeli armed forces which uses Deleuze/Guattari for tactics. They create alternative spaces and openings by just breaking through the walls. The Palestinians do it too by now, my friend Udi Aloni told me." (transcription mine)

from the private space of the subjects (i.e. the host). The roof is that which enables us to hide from God or nature and is as such a life technique, a *techné*, which has the same linguistic root in Greek as the German *Dach*, the roof. Beneath the roof of the host, the laws of the state are only partially applicable. Since we do not believe in imposed laws anymore but in our own projection of the laws, Flusser claims we do not need roofs anymore. He then goes over to a discussion of the wall, which he divides into the outer wall, designed against the foreigner, and the inner wall, designed for the safety of the inhabitants, or rather: prisoners *(Häftlinge)*. The inner wall is made to protect the secret (*Geheimnis*, closely related to *Heim*, home) from the uncanny (*Unheimlichen*). Who cannot stand secrets, he claims, needs to tear down the walls, but everyone else must also poke holes into the walls to be able to look outside. The window thus poked into a wall is what enables us to look outside without getting wet from the rain, which Flusser relates to *theoria*, the riskless and experienceless cognition or perception *(Erkennen)*. "Roof, wall, window and door are presently not operational anymore," he maintains and adds a little later that the wires connecting our house can also be made into bundles instead of webs and thus become fascist as opposed to dialogic. He proposes a new architecture, an architecture that attracts the field of human relationships. We will repeat the excerpt quoted above: "Such an attractive house would have to collect relationships, process them into information, store and relay them. A creative [schöpferisch] house as node of the interhuman web."[331] The house he envisions would be an architecture without roof or wall and only built of reversible windows and doors: an architecture without *arcus* or *tectum*. The only feature of architecture Flusser does not mention and hence does not disqualify as dysfunctional is the floor, the ground. Such a house would not offer shelter

---

331 Flusser, Medienkultur, 162.

anymore and would be the end of hospitality. It would be the end of the friend/enemy or the host/guest opposition, and would thus preclude any necessity of filtering. One could not hide anymore from God, the state or the foreigner, which would, according to Flusser, be the end of the master/subject opposition but far from expecting an anarchic natural state where everyone fights everyone else, he believes that people could not do anything but reach out for each other's hands.

Even though apparently contradicting Derrida's notions of hospitality in that he undermines the very concept of hospitality, Flusser's house without walls and roof attempts to re-establish, or at least give an architecture or a structure or a name to that which would attain to the very possibility of impossible or absolute hospitality and at the same time gives us a metaphor for the argument we tried to make in the chapter entitled "Communication as life". When all of us are equal in that we cannot retreat, Flusser seems to say, then we will realise that we belong to an infinite and indefinite web of relationships; these houses would be weblike projectors for alternative [read: virtual] worlds common to all mankind [read: common to all].[332] Flusser knows very well of the danger of such a project, of the endangerment of our minds and bodies but he claims that it would be much more dangerous not to wage it and remain forever between four porous walls, beneath a perforated roof in front of our television. His house without walls must be taken as a metaphor if we are not to move mankind to areas of the world that accommodate our skin without fur. It is, and he points to that himself, a metaphor for our mindset in relation to the others, of our perception of the world and our own place in it, of how to deal with communication going to and fro our house, read: mind. It is also an attack on the detachment of *theoria*, the safe knowledge to be obtained standing at the window looking outside.

332   Ibid., 163.

The house without walls calls for a new contestation of balance, which, as we have argued above, always implies dance and danger. When he writes that we would reach out for each other's hands he evokes an image of the round dance, the Dionysian celebration of the community.

What is the relationship of such architecture and community to the notion of hospitality? It is precisely because there is no home in the traditional sense, *no home which produces the stranger*, that there is no stranger anymore. Hence, there is no one to offer the gift of hospitality to, which is the very condition for absolute hospitality or the absolute gift to take place: there is no knowing of the gift of hospitality, neither on the side of the sovereign (who has then become inexistent) nor on the side of the host (who also would not exist). The disappearance of the notion of hospitality is the prerequisite that the unknowable, unknown, unintentional, unconditional, anonymous gift, the gift which in the end translates into the gift of unconditional and asymmetric love, may actually take place. Flusser calls for our involvement and engagement with the world on creative terms and he appears convinced that it is the symmetric connection of all nodes running together in our house (mind) which is the prerequisite for such a creative engagement with the world.

4.2.4 The windowless monad

The windowless monad in its most basic conception may appear to be the counterpart to the house without walls. To begin with, we may imagine a house that has no windows and no doors, a cube perhaps with no entry or exit point. It appears the monad is a bunker that has been closed from the outside, or rather, that has never been opened. The idea of the monad is a little more complex, however, and above all more porous. The monad, according to Gottfried Wilhelm Leibniz who coined the term, is a simple substance, the element of things, the atom of nature.[333] Thus, the monads have always existed, they have no beginning or end in a natural cause (§4–5) but rather through an act of creation or annihilation (§6) by God. They cannot be divided into parts (§3) since they already are the smallest elements which can only make connections to other monads to enter into composites. Monads are in a way autistic entities:

> There is also no way of explaining how a monad can be altered or changed internally by some other creature, since one cannot transpose anything in it, nor can one conceive of any internal motion that can be excited, directed, augmented, or diminished within it, as can be done in composites, where there can be change among the parts [...] Thus, neither substance nor accident can enter a monad from without.[334]

This does not mean that the monad does not undergo change. Since nothing can enter into the monad, Leibniz proposes that there is an inner principle (§11) which guides these inner changes: "The human soul is imagined as a monad, as an entity closed in itself, as a house without windows and doors, in which the supposedly outer world is only actualised as inner conception."[335] The activity of this inner principle is called desire (Begehren, appetition, §15). Not only are perceptions (which he divides into normal perceptions [perceptio] as well as conscious perceptions [apperceptio], §14) a quality exclusive of simple substances, they are also the only thing to be found in simple substances (§17). The monads are connected by a predetermined harmony, which,

---

333   Leibniz, Monadologie, 11. The paragraphs indicated in this chapter refer to the paragraphs of Monadology.
334   Leibniz, The Principles of Philosophy, or, the Monadology, 285.
335   Schlüter, Die Falte zwischen Leib und Seele.

according to Leibniz, is stabilised in God's creation of the best of possible worlds, the perfect agreement of all things created (§56). The inner world of the monad is an image of the universe, and the only thing of which it has a clearer image than the universe is its body that intricately belongs to it. As the soul perceives its body, it perceives the universe (§62). The soul follows its laws of final causes and the body its laws of active causes and they meet in the prestabilised harmony since they are images of the same universe (§78–79). Gilles Deleuze illustrates the connection between body and soul as a baroque house made of two stories: the first story, the body or organism, does have windows corresponding to the five senses, while the upper part, the soul or monad, is receptive to the senses but is in itself a closed entity decorated with wallpaper subdivided by folds.[336]

According to Deleuze, body and soul are strictly speaking separated. The criterion or the operative concept of that division is that of the fold, a fold which runs between the upper and lower story and may be indefinitely folded without ever cancelling out the distinction between body and soul. There are souls on the ground floor of the house too, and it is reason which summons some of them to ascend to the second floor. The fold is continued in the unfolding: "The unfolding is not the opposite of the fold but follows the fold to the next fold."[337] It is a continuous folding-unfolding-refolding (a fold is always between two other folds[338]), whereby organisms have endogenous folds and inorganic matter has exogenous folds.[339] Each monad is a singularity representing the world, its world. The monad reaches out to the world: "Since the world is in the monad, each comprises the entire series of states (*Zustände*) of the world; since however the monad is for the world, none comprises in an obvious form the 'ground' (basis: *Grund*) of

---

336 Deleuze, Die Falte, 13.
337 Ibid., 16.
338 Ibid., 28.
339 Ibid., 18.

the series, from which they all result and which remains external to them like the principle of their harmony."[340] Elsewhere: "One has to set the world into the subject for this subject to be for the world."[341]

The monad strongly resembles the brain as biology knows it today and, as conceived by Leibniz and Deleuze, is interesting for a number of reasons. First, they stress the absolute singularity of every monad. Second, the monad opens a gradual field of perceptions, from normal to conscious perceptions (apperceptions) which indicate that the singular monad, even though to a certain degree streamlined by an eternal, preestablished harmony, bears a certain responsibility of its inner projection. Third, it does away with a clear-cut division between body and soul without denying that they are separate. The monad is porous to a certain degree and it is so through its senses. The senses, that is, the ground floor, is the filter for what is perceived on the second floor. While Flusser's home without walls creates a symmetrical structure for giving and receiving in response to the technological challenges the home faces today and is so able to abolish the idea of hospitality in favour of absolute, unknown hospitality, he does not propose a filter, a technological or organic filter and is willing to risk an endless stream of information. What the windowless monad and the home without walls have in common is the idea of reaching out, albeit in a different way. Flusser seems to envision a being-with-others-for-the-world, while Deleuze seems to suggest a being-with-oneself-for-the-world. It is not entirely clear where Deleuze and Leibniz situate the media, those filters and catalysers external to us, but it appears that it is not a major concern for the model of the monad which focuses on the perception of singularities somehow detached from the world but still reaching out for it.

---

340   Ibid., 47.
341   Ibid., 48.

4.2.5   Conclusion

We looked at three types of architecture of the home: the castle, the home without walls and the windowless monad. These mark the cornerstones of our perception of our perception though it must be conceded that a more adept opposition to the home without walls might have been the bunker. There is an entire body of functional types of architecture, those companions of man since primeval times[342], which could be treated as metaphors for our mind and the filters separating our mind from the environment: hotels, nests, prisons, restaurants, hospitals, nightclubs, museums, movie theatres, tents, motor homes, earth holes, camps, skyscrapers, brothels, submarines, tree houses, caves, airports, trains, backpacks, cars, hard drives, internets, couches, yachts, igloos, libraries, shopping malls, ant hills. We explicitly read them as metaphors, also in view of Luciana Martinelli and Marco Testi's remarks, namely that the castle has become a cultural topos of the occident that hardly represents historic reality.[343] What is common to them is the idea of dwelling, which, to refer to Heidegger again, points to thinking.[344] Each in its own way poses the question of the relation of the community to the self, and each has a different way of dealing with it, but they all have in common that these questions are posed in terms of the sovereign, filters, responsibility, and hospitality.

The castle, although it is a hyperbole, is perhaps that which is closest to the common perception of the home and the mind today. It is a heavily armed structure, and most of these arms are passive

---

342   Benjamin, Illuminations, 239.
343   Martinelli, "Il nuovo castello dell'occidente: il simbolismo del castello nella narrativa contemporanea", 383; Testi, "Il castello del diavolo, l'abbazia di Babilonia.", 389. In: Arena et al. (Eds.), Monastero e castello nella costruzione del paesaggio.
344   Heidegger, Building, Dwelling, Thinking, in: Basic Writings.

filters, that is, arms for defence, such as walls, towers and moats. Today's obsession with filters to keep that away from us which we do not want has turned into resignation that any other defence, which might include offence, is possible or desirable.[345] Flusser, as we have seen, solves the issue by abolishing all defensive structures, by abolishing the secret even, which for Derrida is important, especially in the last chapter of *The Gift of Death*. Leibniz and Deleuze, on the other hand, refer to the filters built into every porous monad, our senses, which are so much tied to the body that it is that which we best know. We can conclude these ruminations on the architectures of the home, that the essential activity of perception is that of reaching out rather than closing in. The difficulty in dealing with advertising is, however, that it is usually not us who reach out to the other but the other who reaches out to us. Whenever such reaching out appears to be a reaching out that withdraws as soon as we do not reply in the way intended by the other, we ought to become suspicious.

4.3   The disappearing sovereign

The notion of the sovereign in relation to existing structures or boundaries is a fickle one. If the sovereign is she who does not depend on anything else in order to be the ruler (who is able to suspend the rules), in what way can we still speak of a sovereign when we accept an internally preestablished harmony or an interrelatedness of all being? Can the notion of independence be upheld, and if so, where does the sovereign territory end?

---

345   The German *Bundesamt für Sicherheit und Informationstechnik*, for instance, dedicates the entire book on anti-spam strategies only to filtering. Topf, J. "Antispam-Strategien: unerwünschte E-Mails erkennen und abwehren" Köln: Bundesanzeiger Verlag, 2005.

If we stay for a moment with the house or the home, is it not obvious how the sovereign has disappeared? In our cultures, the sovereign used to be the patriarch, but the patriarch, in order to exist, needed his people and his space, the family and the house, the herd and the hearth. After we have witnessed the disintegration of the traditional nuclear family, the disintegration of the hearth naturally followed. The family was replaced by more modern, nomadic, temporal forms of cohabitation which embrace the new requirements of the emancipated self, the self that is let go from the duties of holding the house. Since the home became less populated and the traditional home cook, usually the mother or the wife, assumed other duties outside of the household, the microwave and precooked food consumed in front of the *Ersatz*-family of the television or in the *Ersatz*-home of the car replaced the hearth, as the lament of culture critique goes. The patriarch knows, but forgets, Derrida says, that there is no body without the graft of culture,[346] this culture that made the patriarch a patriarch. With the shift to a more nomadic life form, the patriarch has no physical territory to call his own. He has to share his house with his family, or what remains of it, each member of which is another petty sovereign who has a say in who or what may enter the house. He also has to share his home with a telephone, a computer hooked to the Internet and a letterbox, and has to endure noise entering the home from below, above and all sides, noise which—unseen and untouchable—trespasses the boundaries of the former sovereign territory. And finally, thanks to mobile forms of work (laptop, telephones, Internet) the sovereign has to share his house with his workplace.

The home's sovereign is also subjected to the sovereignty of the state in which the house stands. The sovereignty that is hierarchically higher placed is most often one that limits the sovereignty

---

346 Derrida, *The Politics of Friendship*, 185.

of the sovereign of the house and not one that broadens her rights. In the hierarchy of sovereignty, from cells to cosmos, each sovereign only has freedom of movement or decision already delineated by those higher in the hierarchy. If the petty sovereign of the home breaks the state law within the home, it is only because, as argued before, the state has reserved this area for private trespasses and will, generally speaking, intervene only upon complaint or suspicion.

If we subscribe to the natural interrelatedness of all things, as outlined in the chapter "Communication as life", we have a difficult time accepting the notion of the sovereign as the sovereign over somebody, and if we do accept such a notion, it would have to be a mutual, omnidirectional sovereignty that gives us a sense of responsibility for ourselves and for others. We have hinted at hierarchies of sovereignty, but each of these sovereign positions requires bodies to be sovereign over, and it is only due to these bodies that the sovereign exists at all. Thus, the hierarchy may also be turned upside down to say that there is no sovereign if her subjects do not behave accordingly and if she is not able to expel them from her territory. One is no longer sovereign over one's body if some cells decide to form a cancer which one cannot remove. One is only sovereign as long as one's subjects are willing to endure one's sovereignty, thus, it could be argued that the real sovereigns—those that enable the sovereignty in the first place—are the subjects to be ruled.

The sovereign is tied to the question of property. Shifts in the perception of what property means is a further cause for the erosion of the sovereign. Today, we can see a divide between harsher laws protecting intellectual property—often criticised and still succumbed to[347]—, and the willing contribution of information

---

347   The British street artist (or artist collective) Banksy made a point about this
      in the 2005 book "Wall and Piece": the usual copyright notice starts with the

that explicitly waives copyrights in whole or in parts. There are not only forms of property modelled on the traditional "this is mine" but forms of right to use, such as the rent or lease, which, for the time of the right to use, confuse the distinction between rightful owner and rightful user. All said, we can observe that the erosion of the sovereign is an erosion, even an impossibility, insofar as we cannot determine her territory, her term of office or her subjects any longer, if we were ever able to do so. The notion of the sovereign requires clear distinctions and when these blur, she cannot lay claim to her sovereignty in relation to space, time or subjects.

In a seminar held at the Paris satellite of the European Graduate School, Derrida speaks about forgiveness.[348] He says that forgiveness is a *sovereign* act. Thus, the sovereign is she who can forgive. Paradoxically—it is Derrida speaking after all—we can only forgive the unforgivable. If we forgive that which we are able to forgive, we do not forgive. Only that which cannot be forgiven can be forgiven, but it cannot, since it is the unforgivable. The mechanisms are the same as those we observed with the gift and hospitality: Derrida is going after the pure and unconditional. He says that true forgiveness takes place between one singular irreplaceable person to another singular irreplaceable person. With this parenthesis he already—and perhaps rightly—excludes the forms of communication which we have set out to analyse: those based on exchangeability. At the same time, he gives us a means of pinning down the recipient in his or her self-understanding as someone irreplaceable. In the Paris seminar, Schirmacher's objection was that one can only forgive oneself. With this turn, he brings the sovereign back to the only territory which is truly hers: herself. When

---

disclaimer "Copyright is for losers©™" and is followed by "Against his better judgement Banksy has asserted his right under the Copyright, Designs and Patents Act" etc.

348   The seminar is electronically available at http://www.youtube. com/profile_favorites?user=egsvideo&p=r&page=5.

there is no sovereign in the traditional sense, no sovereign *over* others, the sovereign remains with herself and it is only by this se-cret act of self-forgiveness, for it must not enter an economic cycle, that forgiveness can actually take place. Still, true forgiveness can only take place in forgiving ourselves the unforgivable, and such a coming to terms with oneself or one's unforgivable deeds is a pre-requisite for leading a fulfilled life. Schirmacher's *homo generator,* which we will term *generans* for a number of reasons outlined below, "concerns the whole person and embraces embodiment and communal action as well."[349] *Generans* has a general attitude of openness, of letting go and thus does not imposing itself upon others to the point of obsessing or possessing them.

---

349 Schirmacher, Homo Generator in Artificial Life, 87.

5 The challenge of productivity

One of the indications of a healthy economic sector is a constant increase in production over time. The term "production" derives from Latin *producere*, which first of all means to bring forth or to manufacture. Productivity, defined as the output generated per unit of input, is the measurand of production at a determined time. Thus, with an input of 1 unit and an output of 1.5 units, the productivity is positive. The question of marginal productivity concerns the optimisation of resources where a determined input has the greatest per unit output.

One line of argument held in chapter 1 holds equally true for a critique of productivity the way it is dealt with in daily business. Input and output are often—for lack of a better option—quantified in a monetary equivalent: an input of $100 versus an output of $150. Using money as unit for measuring input and output allows for an inclusion of various factors such as labour, real estate, raw materials, machinery, promotion etc. but it bears the danger that any of these contributing factors are not rightly quantified and it tends to exclude factors that do not enter the company's balance sheet. Furthermore, especially with ecologically problematic substances, the inclusion of most or all factors and their quantification may lead to an attitude that it is right to pollute if only the proper market price is paid for it.

The definition of productivity lacks however an innate generational thinking as it is only concerned with the ratio between microeconomic input and output at a determined time. The main challenges with a simplified understanding of the term "productivity" have been tackled by economists with various changes or additions to the *productivity = output / input* equation.

Stockflow analysis and input-output sheets are common instruments in economy, ecology and materials logistics. Stockflow analysis is based on the first theorem of thermodynamics according to which the energy/mass balance in a determined system remains stable.[350] Ideally, a complete stockflow analysis would take into mathematical account all flows and end up with a balanced input/output ratio.[351] It thus presupposes the choice of a specific system and a choice of substances whose input and output are measured. Stockflow analysis is an instrument that measures processes as opposed to states. In practice the problem arises with the very inclusion of energy and mass since the exhausting measurement of all stock flows is—for economic reasons and for reasons of correct measurement—hardly feasible.[352] To understand the ecologic impact of a product or a process, stockflow analysis is combined with the output/input sheet and the product's ecologic lifecycle.

> The ecologic product lifecycle ideally contains the phases of extraction of raw materials, production, use and disposal/recycling of a product, including the transportation between these phases. The input in resources and the output of emissions are collected separately per process observed and finally added for the entire product.[353]

As Braungart and McDonough stress, what is given back to the ecologic cycle must be uncontaminated for the biosphere to be

---

350   Siegenthaler, Ökobilanz, 30–1.
351   Ibid., 31.
352   Ibid.
353   Ibid., 33.

able to use it as a productive force. The goal is to design products in such a way that contamination does not take place. They define two metabolisms, the organic (biological) and the technical metabolism. These must be held separately in the production and degeneration of a product to avoid the contamination and thus deterioration of either metabolic process.[354]

To use such an approach for the mental environment appears problematic. The very process of interchange of meaning is such that the meaning changes and will most likely never return to its original, uncontaminated form. In the mental sphere, we will also call productivity the difference between input and output but be aware that certain meanings will change with time and usage and it is up to historians and etymologists to remind us of the initial meaning. The contamination that we need to be cautious of is that of different systems, such as instrumentalised uses of particular words or mental concepts in the political or economic sphere (e.g. targets of opportunity, freedom, Aryan, *Volk*). The instrumentalisation is inevitable but the degree of instrumentalisation, the usage and the connotations linked to it may become fatal to a sustainable or ethical development of both systems (linguistic and economic or political) as we tried to demonstrate in chapter 1 with the notion of "freedom of speech". We can thus see that it is not so much the connotations *per sé* we need to be aware of, as the connections to other nodes that may be cut off without building other equally valid connections.[355]

---

354 Braungart and McDonough, Einfach intelligent produzieren, 135ff.
355 National socialism has twisted many concepts and pieces of art and cut off connections without establishing equally valid other connections. Due to their alleged or confirmed proximity to national socialism, works by Wagner, Heidegger and Schmitt, to name but a few, had a problematic reception after World War II. Likewise, works by Jewish authors, philosophers or artists were dismissed in the Third Reich, their connections or validity undermined so that their reception in that region became problematic or outlawed.

To recapitulate, we may state in general that *productivity = output / input*. The challenge of productivity lies in the choice and measurement of productive factors according to an ethical framework, the correct measurement and the relation to future productivity of the system measured and those related to it. The turning point of productivity—where productivity becomes negative—is the point where productivity undermines itself.

5.1 Unproductivity as the mode of economy

It was observed earlier that the advertising complex from a general point of view is the driving force of an economy of excess: one market participant—in order to outdo its competition—spends as much as possible on a potlatch, a gift which then obliges the opponent to answer with another potlatch to outdo the former market participant. In order to maintain the ability of gift-giving, the particular economy of the market participant, which is an economy of scarcity, needs to be taken into account. The ultimate goal of potlatch is, according to Bataille, the ultimate gift which cannot be surpassed and amounts to death. The gift of death in the general economy of excess can however only take place when the economy of scarcity of the particular system is not taken into account.

Following the definition of productivity as output divided by input, we can define unproductivity as an excess of input versus output. Due to the difficulty arising from the measurement of input (material, labour etc.) and output (finished product, emissions etc.), we can only in rare cases correctly determine the overall balance sheet of a particular product across all systems involved. There are cases, particularly with products that are detrimental to the environment, where the input in monetary terms would greatly exceed the output if all factors were taken into account.

The notion of unproductivity as an excess of input versus output is somewhat misleading since there is still an output, hence there is still production. Thus we are urged to think of unproductivity as the undermining of productivity, that is, as that which prevents future productivity. Productivity must be thought of in terms of productivity and not in terms of monetary or material input in and output of a particular system.

In the advertising complex, the productivity equation can be looked at on different levels. The big picture takes into account all resources going into the production and promotion of a product and the return derived from the sales. The outcome of this equation is not necessarily in the hands of the producer since uncontrollable factors that border the system (fashion, media, market, politics) may greatly influence the sales. The question at hand is therefore: what must the output be today so that output is still possible tomorrow?

The case of outdoor advertising in São Paulo serves to illustrate this point.[356] The outdoor advertising industry in São Paulo has for a long time been able to achieve a constant growth by putting up more billboards, many of which without permit. When space on walls became rare, banners were hung up between streetlights or trees, flyers were handed out and airplanes equipped with advertising banners. For a while, the outdoor advertising industry was thus able to generate revenue year after year. Eventually, the citizens/consumers of São Paulo grew annoyed with the proliferation of outdoor advertising and the City Council called for a halt. The rupture introduced prohibited nearly all of the 13,000 billboards across the city, which signifies a reduction of present and possibly future growth for the outdoor industry to zero. Roberto Tripoli,

---

356   See: Rother, in New York Times: Streets Are Paved With Neon's Glare, and
       City Calls a Halt, 12 Dec 2006; Neue Zürcher Zeitung: Das Stadtbild São
       Paulos wird gesäubert, 12 Feb 2007; Moser, in Tages-Anzeiger: Die Stadt
       hinter Reklametafeln hervorgeholt, 24 May 2007.

president of the City Council is quoted in New York Times: "Some people are going to have to pay a price. But things were out of hand, and the population has made it clear it wants this."[357] The City had to expulse billboard advertising. During the era of hospitality, when billboards were guests in and of the city, something has happened which transformed these guests into enemies to be got rid of. In fact, São Paulo has tried in vain for some time to reduce the number of billboards and to not allow for new advertising spaces, but these bylaws were disregarded by the advertising industry and prosecution of illegal outdoor advertising became a burden. In other words: the city of São Paulo tried to limit its hospitality and did not succeed. The sovereign reaction thus became all the more violent, banning largely all advertising spaces. During the era of proliferation of billboards in São Paulo, the sales capacity of a singular billboard diminished with each new advertisement. The competition in the visual field grew to such an extent that people likely did not pay any attention to a particular advertisement. Thus, the productivity in the general economy of billboard advertising (overall output versus overall input) decreased until the City Council called for a rupture. The few outdoor advertisements which are still allowed after the prohibition will have a greater impact on the passers-by—however not always and everywhere.

The São Paulo case is also interesting for a reason that deals with the etymology of "production". The Latin *producere* not only means to put forth or to build or fabricate; it also means to tempt or seduce as well as to show in public and to expand.[358] It seems all these diverse meanings come together in outdoor advertising. Billboards are manufactured to bring forth a characteristic of a particular product in a certain way to seduce those who look at

357   Rother, in New York Times, Streets Are Paved With Neon's Glare, and City Calls a Halt, 12 Dec 2006.
358   Langenscheidt Schulwörterbuch Latein, "produco".

it. Unlike many other types of advertising, it does so exclusively by showing it in and to the public.[359] The São Paulo case indicates that there is a point at which this expansion in public may lead to overkill, to a death of production by overproduction, a death of the gift by giving too much, an end of hospitality by having offered (or conversely: craved or claimed) too much of it. This death is not the death of two competing actors (outdoor company A and outdoor company B) in an enclosed system due to an extraordinary squandering of their riches before the public. The advertising industry would have gone on for another while until there literally would have been no space left and then would have found ways of adding yet more layers of advertising on other, maybe less physical levels. The end of hospitality was induced by the very public the advertising industry sought to impress. The case also indicates the limits and perhaps shortsightedness of the idea of production, a lack of thinking beyond the momentary success. According to the images in the press, the billboards in question were overdimensional, often as large as entire buildings, and while it may not have been illegal to destroy an illegal billboard, it clearly was not possible for those who were confronted by them due to the sheer size and number of the advertisements. The host's helplessness with putting a lid on hospitality turned into xenophobia, a reaction Derrida anticipates:

> Wherever the "home" is violated, wherever at any rate a violation is felt as such, you can foresee a privatizing and even familialist reaction, by widening the ethnocentric and nationalist, and thus xenophobic, circle: not directed against the foreigner as such, but, paradoxically, against the anonymous technological power.[360]

---

359 The industry term for outdoor and indoor advertising is "out-of-home advertising" (OOH).
360 Derrida, Of Hospitality, 53.

A further explanation for the São Paulo billboard ban is to be found in outdoor advertising's failure to address singularities as singularities. Since a billboard (as many other types of advertising) is blind to those whose gaze it captures, it cannot discriminate between them. Hence it is not able to speak in an individual way to passersby and present what truly interests them. It is furthermore unable to perceive a physical reaction and thus cannot hear when the singular spectator does not want to be addressed at all, or not to that extent: it cannot face the impossibility of the decision.

5.2   Generating life

The dominance of the questions of production and productivity in the economic narrative of our days indicates a certain interest in the creation of things, in setting them into the world. Production designs a definite form. It conceives something which in the very act of production is designed only to receive: to receive a certain shape and certain traits. It gives birth to an inert, infertile being. What is produced is not conceived as something which on its own should have the ability to reproduce itself, let alone to reproduce something which is also able to reproduce—in an endless movement towards the open future. As a consequence, production is not able to face the unexpected and the unexpectable. It can only enable the form, not the forming.

Schirmacher draws our attention to the idea of generation with his concept of homo generator. As opposed to productivity, generation thinks of and in life and bridges individual generation and generation of genus or species. Homo generator is we who are responsible for generation: responsible that generation take place and also signing as responsible for that which is generated. "Responsibility also means being able to assume one's guilt and to reject blame for anything you have not caused yourself", he writes.[361] Homo generator has the "immense ability to produce new forms of life and determine the biological as well as the spiritual future of the earth." [362] When he writes "determine the future" he can only refer to determination as that which is first in an endless sequence of events. It is not a determination that imprisons what is generated.

> Homo generator is an open call [Bestimmung], a concept only now beginning to unfold that might well be interrupted, to begin anew, and then perhaps double back. There exists no Homo yet, but rather s/he is a self-fulfilling prophecy. S/he generates her/himself in the most important life techniques, once simply in breathing, sleeping, gathering food, procreating, fighting—today in solar technology as well, in biotechnology, and in the media. There exists for us the force, the power, and the opportunity to generate—that alone is what is referred to by the concept "Homo generator". [363]

It is not entirely clear why this species of the homo is any different from biological and intellectual beings, other than by auto-attribution of responsibility to the former. Homo generator as the juggler of life and media techniques is in itself a self-fulfilling prophecy: there exists no homo generator yet but we all are homo generators. Since homo generator exists only by virtue of a double self-fulfilling prophecy, that of generating and that of assuming responsibility, we will rather name the beings who exert force and upon whom force is exerted *generans*. Generans is these beings as well as the force in itself (the vector) that is exerted. The notion of generans is not gender-specific and not anthropocentric. It bears

---

361 Schirmacher: Homo Generator: Media and Postmodern Technology.
362 Ibid.
363 Schirmacher/Lyotard: Homo Generator in Artificial Life, 91.

justice to the fact that all singularities are able to generate new forms of life and thus determine the future of the earth, that is, to be first in a sequence of events as an actualizer of the virtual. This ability to put things into the world is what Gossage refers to as creativity, and he writes that "[w]hat we call creativity begins with the ability to recognise what is already there."[364] "Recognise" can be read in a modern and an ancient way, both of which are equally justified. To recognise can mean to see what is there, to perceive it. So, in order to recognise, we must have the ability to perceive our environment. In the ancient sense of German *erkennen*, recognise however also means to know, that is, to have intercourse with. Thus, the word "recognise" also refers to the act of insemination or of generation.

The sequence of events the act of generation inaugurates is one-directional, even though this inauguration is itself part of other horizontal and vertical sequences. We can only look ahead, we can only generate into the future. Derrida writes that "each generation must begin again to involve itself [in faith] without counting on the generation before."[365] As a consequence, we only bear responsibility to what lies ahead, in particular to what we generate. When we observe generans as the force of life, we note that it has responsibility already built in—like homo generator—and the name of this responsibility is sustainability.

Generans is the giver of life—of biological and intellectual life—and bridges the notion of production (of setting something into the world that is deprived of its reproductive organs), of reproduction (of setting one more generation of a kind into the world) and of generation (setting an endless number of generating entities into the world). Generans is the measure of creation and should have become the currency of production a long time ago because

364 Gossage, The Book of Gossage, 37.
365 Derrida, The Gift of Death, 80.

real productivity can only be measured in generative terms, where that which generates more life is considered more productive and that which deprives life is considered unproductive.

5.3 Sustainability: the ecology of the mind

The widely known definition of sustainability is that of the Brundtland report from 1987: "Sustainable development meets the needs of the present without compromising the ability of future generations to meet their own needs."[366] It is significant to note that the Brundtland report does not attribute a definite article to "future generations" and that it uses "generations" in the plural. It thus tries to leave the future open and not limit itself to a specific area, time or people. It implies that, if all generations behave sustainably, there will not be an end to humanity. It also implies that it is possible, at least at the time the report was written, that all mankind could meet its present needs if it did so in the right manner.

The Brundtland report was conceived to meet the ecological crisis of natural resources. Their depletion serving the momentary hubris of mankind without considering the needs of future generations was the spark to manifest another world view, one that has been contemplated or acted out by many thinkers and, most of all, by "the common man" in times of scarcity such as during wars. The idea of sustainability is potentially also subject to a secondary hubris: that of assuming that we know what the future generations' needs are. The way out of this impasse is plotted by practitioners of sustainability, such as Braungart and McDonough: sustainability is only such if it makes sure that our ecological footprint equals

---

366 Lexikon der Nachhaltigkeit, "Weltkommission für Umwelt und Entwicklung (Brundtland-Report), 1987".
http://www.nachhaltigkeit.info/artikel/brundtland-report_563.htm.

zero, which in no way contradicts the idea of leaving footprints.[367] They stress nature's exuberant productivity, which shall here be called generativity, and the footprint we leave must only make sure that what we extract is what we give back in unadulterated form. Future generations are to have the same resources in order to decide themselves what to do with them. It is not admissible to define the needs of future generations (if we need petroleum future generations should also be left with enough of it) but to leave that which we extract so they can make their own decisions based solely on the future by means of the effect of their footprints without counting on the generation before.

Wherein lies the difference between the Brundtland defin-ition of sustainability and the ecological footprint? Both aim for the same goal, namely the preservation of life, but the perspective is different. The Brundtland report thinks in terms of scarcity, of generations (those who are to come), of mass (biomass), and of sociey. The idea of the ecological footprint roots in an understand-ing of nature as something that gives exuberantly. This viewpoint is only possible if adds energy to the mass, as Bataille did. The time unit is not that of a generation but that of life, not so much of societal life but of singular life. Only in this way can the Braungart and McDonough say that we have to give back what we extracted

---

367   The ecological footprint is "expressed in global acres (or global hectares in metric measurement). Each of those acres (hectares) corresponds to one acre (hectare) of biologically productive space with world-average produc-tivity. Today, the biosphere has 26.7 billion acres (or 10.8 billion hectares) of biologically productive space corresponding to less than one-quarter of the planet's surface. These 26.7 billion acres (10.8 billion hectares) include 5.7 billion acres (2.3 billion hectares) of productive ocean and 21 billion acres (8.5 billion hectares) of productive land."
http://www.rprogress.org/ecological_footprint/footprint_FAQs.htm
The author has calculated his footprint to be around 4.5, which means that 2.5 planets Earth would be necessary to maintain the global population if everyone lived like him.
http://www.earthday.net/footprint/index.html.

in uncontaminated form. Only with an eternal future does everything sooner or later find back to its uncontaminated form.

Since sustainability starts anew with every generation, that is,
with everything that is generated and has its own ability to generate, sustainability must not only make sure that there is enough for
future generations, it must also make sure that there is enough for
our own generative tasks and duties. It is hardly fair to patronise
future generations when what is at stake is the beginning of generation, which is always in the very instant of presence. To live in
a cosmic sense means to somehow anticipate the cosmos, that is,
the interrelatedness that surrounds us, without laying hands on it
and instrumentalising it. It means to incessantly create new forms
of life that are fertile in their own right. Since we cannot possibly
grasp the future, we cannot grasp that which we breathe life into
(that which we in-vent). We create and then we let go because "the
planning and control of technology ('Technik') is responsible for
the destruction of the environment."[368]

What are we to do with sustainability in the context of hospitality and of advertising and media? The limits of hospitality as
circumscribed by Derrida are those of the inherent aporia. By offering hospitality we must exclude hospitality to others. It is not
possible to offer hospitality to everyone. *The search for sustainability marks the natural and ethical rupture with hospitality in order
to guarantee hospitality.* It does so in three senses. When hospitality is offered, it must have as its ethical horizon future hospitality:
the host's ability to offer hospitality in the future (vertical sustainability of hospitality within the limits of the host's life); the guest's
ability to be offered hospitality in the future (horizontal sustainability of hospitality); and the host's descendants ability to offer
hospitality (vertical sustainability of hospitality within the host's
genealogical line). The guest's descendants' ability to be offered

---

368 Schirmacher, Ereignis Technik, 51.

hospitality is dependent on this vertical sustainability within the host's genealogical line. These three forces are symmetrical in that they are of equal importance to the maintenance of hospitality but they are asymmetric in that each claims its prevalence over the others. Nevertheless, it is possible to unite them as they all strive towards the maintenance of hospitality for the sake of hospitality (which is the same as the rupture with hospitality for the sake of hospitality). What enables us to weigh these interests is "intuition as authentic truth technique",[369] a phrase we intuitively understand but shall not attempt to pin down by explaining it or by attributing any other values than those inherent in its own drive towards generative fulfilment.

Most advertising today, like most media, is unable to face production beyond production.[370] Sustainable thinking, that is, thinking which calls for non-instrumental, non-damaging generation is not jotted down in the masterplan of today's economic ventures— and this is where the great danger of our future lies, a future to which we offer our genes but which is then free to adapt to its own environment. With media we enter a mental sphere in which the physical, material production is of less importance, and increasingly so with electronic information based on a binary code that is indifferent to its combinations to form something which could be called content. Productive thinking instead of generative thinking is not inherent in the nature of media but it is inherent in an instrumentalised approach to media.

---

369   Ibid., 139.
370   An attempt to enable production beyond production in the media is the blog.

6 The self and its brain

"I am the only me I've got," Schirmacher claims.[371] This is not a tautology and much less a law. It is, like *homo generator* and to a lesser degree like *generans*, a self-fulfilling prophecy. If, according to Leibniz, the body is that of which we have a clear idea, clearer even than the idea of our (i.e. each his or her own) universe,[372] then it must surely be here where we have our sovereign territory. After all that has been said, and all that has been left unsaid, it is however evident that the sovereignty over our body is also at stake, and we may refer back to Nietzsche's concern that it is a bad time for thinkers to live amidst the market vendor's hoarse voices. The singular body, to follow Deleuze, is the baroque house where the souls (minds) dwell on the second floor and the senses on the first, and where the latter act as a filter for the former.[373] This is the view we maintained earlier but which now must be broadened to the interrelatedness between body and mind. Mechanistically it appears evident that what we do not perceive cannot enter our mind but there is an opposite movement also, namely the mind which controls our perception. A person who has lived next to a railway line will likely not hear the trains after some time, and a person who has been confronted all his or her life with billboards will likely not perceive them anymore.

---

371 Schirmacher, Homo Generator: Media and Postmodern Technology.
372 Leibniz, Monadologie, §62, 25.
373 Deleuze, Die Falte, 13.

These considerations may lead to the question of what we subconsciously perceive and what subconsciously moulds us, but this question is one that leads to questions of content rather than form and that are researched in other ways. We will therefore limit ourselves to proposing that there is a movement from our senses to our mind and back and the sum of these movements and associated experiences is what constitutes our internal filters.

6.1   Brain, mind, consciousness

The questions of perception and of the body make it necessary to introduce a few distinctions: what is the brain, what is the mind and what is consciousness? In the entry for "Bewusstsein" Hügli and Lübcke translate the term as consciousness *or* mind,[374] a distinction the LEO Online dictionary does not make, translating Bewusstsein as consciousness or awareness.[375] Merriam Webster OnLine gives the following definitions of consciousness:

> **1 a**: the quality or state of being aware especially of something within oneself **b** : the state or fact of being conscious of an external object, state, or fact **c**: awareness; especially : concern for some social or political cause
>
> **2**: the state of being characterized by sensation, emotion, volition, and thought : mind
>
> **3**: the totality of conscious states of an individual
>
> **4**: the normal state of conscious life
>
> **5**: the upper level of mental life of which the person is aware as contrasted with unconscious processes[376]

---

374   Hügli and Lübcke, "Bewusstsein".
375   LEO Deutsch-Englisch, "Bewusstsein".
376   Merriam-Webster OnLine, "Consciousness".

The different meanings the term "consciousness" may assume can thus be forked into two objectives: consciousness of an object external to us and consciousness of one self or one's self, thus an inner working, which may then be rendered as "mind". The matter becomes more complicated when consulting the German translations for "mind", which range, among others, from intention and thought to intellect, soul and sense.[377] If we followed that trajectory and went one step further, translating some of these notions back into English, we would end up at the term "brain". The Oxford Companion to Philosophy makes evident the difficulty of operating with the terms "mind" and "consciousness" delineating the historical and philosophical trajectories they have assumed in the past.[378] The particular problems with the question of the mind it outlines are 1) characterising the mind; 2) the mind-body problem; 3) mental causation; 4) intentionality; 5) consciousness; and 6) the question of the person.[379]

In a movement to avoid these terms, Catherine Malabou dismisses the question of the brain and consciousness ("Today, it does not matter anymore to ask oneself whether brain and consciousness are one and the same [...]"[380]) in order to favour the question of the *consciousness of the brain*. She does not go to great lengths to explain what her concept of consciousness is but we should be able to understand the phrase "consciousness of the brain" as that which relates the mind to the brain. It is a form of self-awareness of the brain that cannot exactly be grasped but is not out of reach either and may assume the form of a self-fulfilling prophecy. Gossage defines awareness as the "becoming conscious that there

---

377   LEO Deutsch-Englisch, "mind".
378   Oxford Companion to Philosophy, "mind", "mind, history of the philosophy of", "mind, problems of the philosophy of".
379   Ibid., "mind, problems of the philosophy of"
380   Malabou, Was tun mit unserem Gehirn? 7f.

is something bigger controlling us than we have thought."[381] If it is bigger than we have thought, it means we cannot entirely grasp it, but it does not mean we cannot grasp it at all or find our place in it.

As *brain* we understand the biological entity located under our skull, some 20 billion neurons,[382] 100 billion nerve cells with 100 trillion synapses.[383] The exact location of the brain does not matter much especially as neuroscience has discovered that certain thinking does not appear to be located in the head, in that biological organ called brain. As mind we refer to the upper level of Deleuze's baroque house, that which he sometimes calls soul.

What these terms have in common is that they all refer to a singular entity and not to a collective or a multi-headed organism even though it is conceded that the brain, consciousness and the mind are continuously shaped by a multitude of intra-, inter- and extrapersonal events or entities. Even without having clarified the terms of consciousness and mind in an exhaustive, clear-cut manner, something others have failed at before, we should intuitively or even intellectually be able to understand what is at stake.

6.2   Plasticity and flexibility

It is the shaping of the brain that is the main concern of Malabou's text *Was tun mit unserem Gehirn?* ("Que faire de notre cerveau?": What to do with our brain?). According to ample neuroscientific evidence, the brain is a plastic[384] organ and Malabou argues that it is the notion of plasticity which can bridge the various

---

381   Gossage, The Book of Gossage, 37.
382   Malabou, Was tun mit unserem Gehirn? 31.
383   Informationsdienst Wissenschaft, "Brain-Imaging: Faszinierende Forschungen verändern Psychiatrie nachhaltig".
384   *plassein* (Greek): to model, to form.

neurosciences.[385] Plasticity has two correlated significations: the ability to be formed and the ability to form.[386] Thus, the notion of plasticity speaks a clear language with regards to causation admitting that something can simultaneously be cause and effect in an endless movement of mutual formation. It bridges the notion of passivity and activity and—assuming the idea of a consciousness of the brain—is able to reinforce the notion of responsibility of and for the self within certain limits of biological development.

Plasticity is in sharp contrast to the notions of flexibility and of elasticity. Elasticity is the ability to deform and invariably return to the prior form. As such it is of little interest to this argument. Flexibility, on the other hand, shall be contrasted more clearly with the idea of plasticity, since it is a term which has unfortunately and inadvertently become fashionable, especially in the narrative of Western economics, to designate a state of existence or consciousness that allows oneself to be shaped. Flexibility is a purely reactionary idea, a conformation or adjustment to environmental factors or such determined by those in power. It may be said that the idea of flexibility—a term often used with reference to the ability of a person to work under a set of conditions, even when these conditions are in flux—grew out of the paradigm of one-directional communication or power-relationships. It is the poor man's plasticity, the ability to be formed without the ability to form this formation: "Flexibility is plasticity minus its genius."[387] It is thus the misleading promise of sovereignty, of being on top of things, designed to inject some sort of self-confidence into the subjects that are ruled.

The antagonistic, creative forces at work in plasticity are tamed in the notion of flexibility to indicate that some sort of harmony

---

385   Malabou, Was tun mit unserem Gehirn? 12.
386   Ibid., 13.
387   Ibid., 24.

can be achieved if the subject is flexible enough to allow for it. This harmony is not a pre-established harmony, not a mutual, symmetrical harmony, but a one-sided asymmetric adjustment to what is given; an adjustment that, when practiced enough, becomes automatic. Advertising, according to McLuhan, is one of these "crude" attempts to automate society.[388]

"Democracy can only be its own formation; it has no given form."[389] What Nancy says of democracy is also true for plasticity but not for flexibility: Flexibility has a given form although this form takes on different shapes: it is given by that to which one behaves flexibly. Plasticity, on the other hand, is itself a forming of the form and requires something which can loosely be termed consciousness. It does not depend on any pre-established form. It is, like balance as outlined above, and like dance, a contestation of differences, an interplay of will, action, reaction: a clash of forces or a possibility of identities. It takes the momentum and transforms it: "To claim true plasticity of the brain amounts to the question what the brain can do and not only what it can endure."[390] It indicates the space for improvisation in relation to genetic necessity,[391] a question similar to the one Badiou worked at trying to find—using logic—the space in which freedom—and thus creation—in a fully determined environment is possible.[392] Plasticity designates the transformations that take place between the determined and the open form.[393] Flexibility on the other hand takes the momentum and transforms the subject.

388   McLuhan, Understanding Media, 227.
389   Nancy, "Art, Community, Freedom", Seminar at European Graduate School, 11 June 2007.
390   Malabou, Was tun mit unserem Gehirn? 25.
391   Ibid., 18.
392   Badiou, seminar at European Graduate School, August 2006.
393   Malabou, Was tun mit unserem Gehirn? 49.

6.3   The plasticities of the brain

The brain's plasticity refers to the ability to form neural connections, to activate and deactivate synapses but also to intensify or weaken these connections. This is not a purely *mental* process: it is reflected on a microscopic scale in the *physical* development of the brain. The functional patterns this plasticity follows are divided into the plasticity of development (the modelling of neural connections); the plasticity of modulation (modification of neural connections throughout the life); and the plasticity of regeneration (the ability to regenerate, to repair or heal damaged neural connections, for instance after a lesion).[394]

The *plasticity of development*[395] designates the formation of the brain's general neural structures and lasts about fifteen years. This development takes place according to genetic determination, a pre-programmed code, and determines the physical growth of the brain. As a metaphor we may imagine the sculptor who sees the shape of the sculpture in the granite or marble block. Despite the determinism we still call this formation plasticity because it refers to the creation of synaptic connections *and* their modelling. The plasticity ruled by genetic determinism becomes weaker with time and begins to go over to a modelling in relation to our own activity and environment.

The *plasticity of modulation*[396] designates the modification of neural connections by modulation of synaptic efficiency and may be called the history of the brain. It is tied to the experiences of the singularity, its life and interactions. By repetition the brain relocates, modifies or transforms synapses. This is a double mechanism: on the one hand, the plasticity of modulation strengthens

---

394   Ibid., 13–14.
395   For this paragraph, see: Malabou, Was tun mit unserem Gehirn? 31–36.
396   For this paragraph, see: Malabou, Was tun mit unserem Gehirn? 36–42.

those synapses that are repeatedly activated, and on the other hand, it weakens those that are not used very often. We may liken this to the continuous modification of codes, for instance binary codes, according to the frequency of occurrence of the single constituents of the code.[397] These modifications not only lead to the strengthening or weakening of synapses, they may also shape and enlarge entire areas of the brain. While human brains develop similarly in the phase of development, each singular brain differs greatly from the point of view of its history.

The *plasticity of regeneration*[398] is divided into two processes: the regeneration of old cells (secondary neurogenesis), which however does not appear to cover all areas of the brain, and the ability to compensate certain deficits that were caused by an injury. Even though some injuries are irreparable, the brain—at least in the beginning—tries to reorganise synapses in novel ways so as to compensate for lost functions. Malabou cites a case where a man had lost his hands and received hand transplantation four years later. The phantom pain vanished and the man was able to use his new hands. The brain thus was able to renew the idea of hands. Secondary neurogenesis, that is the regeneration of old cells, is not found in all areas of the brain. Especially in lower brain functions, such as vision, it is not found, while it appears to exist in higher functions, such as those activated for learning or for memory. This explains why we are still able to learn up to a high age.

Plasticity is not only a rejuvenating and modifying force. In dependence of the requirements and experiences, the brain is also able to destroy parts of itself, such as a certain memory, to cut off

---

397   The Morse alphabet, for instance, reserves shorter sequences of dots and dashes for letters that are more frequently used (E = ·). The computer keyboard groups those letters that are more often used closer to the standard finger position. Consequently, the arrangement of keys varies slightly according to the language.

398   For this paragraph, see: Malabou, Was tun mit unserem Gehirn? 42–48.

connections to favour others. It is able to sacrifice parts of itself for something that appears more relevant for survival or more congruent with past experiences that are expected to be returning in the future. The aim is to reduce the required time for processes of consciousness, so that the body appears to act independently.[399] The applications of this are numerous and corporeal automation is usually acquired by processes of repetition and training, such as learning (and forgetting) to drive a car, to play a musical instrument, to play sports. Repetition, or its most extreme form: the drill, can in this respect be seen as neural streamlining. Repetition may however "bore" the brain after some time, which then requires something different, more exciting. Virilio quotes the neurologist Didier Vincent saying that the brain does not like to be bored, hence it gets high on sports, sex, leisure activities and so on.[400] The bored brain thus longs for the carnival, which every sensible sovereign grants it in order to make sure that the subject (or the brain) keeps enduring the flexibility asked of it.

What is the significance of these findings for an ethics of communication? Malabou notes that the notion of plasticity has an aesthetic (sculpture), an ethic (providence, care, repair) and a political dimension (responsibility in the double movement of giving and accepting form).[401] The most salient point of the scientific evidence of the plasticity of the brain is perhaps that the brain is not a static entity. It is a continuously changing neural network and not a centralised structure; a network that is constantly adapting to the environment and to the experiences we make. While at first it may appear that this is a question of a change of software, it is really the hardware that undergoes transformation throughout our lives. During the phase of development, the brain grows in

---

399 Virilio, Die Eroberung des Körpers, 103.
400 Ibid., 102.
401 Malabou, Was tun mit unserem Gehirn? 50.

mass and the plasticities of modification and regeneration have also a physical effect on the synapses and neurons. It is this which we called a growth in organic intelligence in the chapter entitled "Communication as life". The network of the brain is not a network where every node is touching another by means of connections. The neural network is characterised by synapses *not* touching each other and never being one with each other. These gaps between synapses, the void space between sending and receiving is where Malabou locates the random, the surprising that "sketches the scope of action of plasticity."[402]

Closely related to this first point is the second point: the forces at work in shaping the structure of the brain are not one but several. Sometimes they may be antagonistic, such as when the plasticity of development is acting out the genetic programme while the plasticity of modification depending on our lives' experiences already tries to alter the structure. These plastic forces, even the destructive ones, have however one common goal, which is securing the life of the brain. The three plasticities thus from a type of autoimmune system which strives for longevity. The forces in these systems are symmetric in that each of it has an equal status in its irreplaceable microscopic role in forming the whole. Thus, this symmetry of forces corresponds to a three-sided asymmetry.

The third point, which is completed with the plasticity of modification, is that each brain is a singular entity. No two brains have the same physiological structure, hence every sensory stimulus is processed or perceived in a different way. The singularity of the brain makes us expect that it is impossible to trigger the exact same neural reaction in two persons. This should account for different tastes and corresponds with the everyday experience that the same stimulus may trigger reactions at polar opposites in two persons.

---

402   Ibid., 56.

The fourth point is that the brain has some capacity to let go. It is able to destroy itself or parts of itself. It does not fervently accumulate memory but it sets this memory in relation to what it expects to be of relevance and lets go of what is not needed, or at least, relegates it to an archive where it may be found again under certain circumstances. It practices a kind of letting-go towards itself.

The fifth point is that the brain appears to have the ability to reflect on itself and act accordingly. Even though we may not be conscious of our brain and the plastic processes that are taking place in it, it can do so on its own; it is thus to a certain degree a windowless monad. Like the windowless monad, the pre-established harmony between the monads may in a metaphorical sense be found in the brain's phase of development when it is formed in much the same way as other humans' brains while remaining open to the sensory world. To say that the brain does not depend on our consciousness of it does not mean that we need not be conscious of it or that it does not depend on us. When we choose to learn to play the piano, we choose an activity that forms and reforms our brain and along with it our mental structure.

When we talked about balance as the paradigm of communication, we noted how communication must search for an equilibrium but how it is not the equilibrium that is actually the aim. It is rather the search itself, the contestation between forces. This is equally true for the brain. It must search but not find the balance between determination and freedom, between forming and being formed, between maintenance and explosion. Malabou writes that "only by producing explosives can life give its freedom a form, that is, turn away from determinism."[403] She goes on to saying that it is this explosion that is also a rupture, the passage from one state to the next or one disposition to the next, which is where she locates

---

403   Ibid., 108.

the metamorphosis from the neural to the mental and concludes that identity opposes its own becoming to the degree it forms itself.[404] This consciousness of the brain as the passage from the neural to the mental is the fourth plasticity Malabou names, one that has not been the objective of neurosciences. In the end, she calls for a readiness for explosion, for non-terrorist explosions such as those of anger:

> To ask: 'What to do with our brain?' surely and above all means to consider the possibility to say no to a miserable political, economic, but also medial culture that does nothing but celebrate the victory of flexibility and to hallow the domination of obedient individuals whose only merit is that they know how to lower their heads cheerfully.[405]

If communication is life and if there is only one world in which to live, then we understand that every vital force is plastic[406] and that this plasticity is the form, or rather: the forming of the form of this world.[407] It then also becomes evident that certain formings of forms, namely those that form asymmetrically without allowing to be formed themselves, cannot be adequately called a representation of life, and it is not surprising that these forms are not intuitively recognised as of one's own kind by that which lives.

---

404   Ibid., 109–110.
405   Ibid., 116.
406   Ibid., 108.
407   Ibid., 60.

7 Towards responsiveness in and in confrontation of advertising

This study follows three general trajectories: "market logic", which in parts corresponds to economic theory; biology, biosemiotics and ecology; and Derrida's deconstruction of cultural or linguistic aporias. We set out to understand today's issues with the advertising complex since advertising is not only a major economic engine but also aims at occupying our minds in some way. The contraposition of advertising, biology and cultural aporias reveals a fundamental discrepancy between their respective internal logics and their founding paradigms.

The most salient point is that the market logic is unable to face the irreplaceable, unique, singular being it addresses. This is the same issue with mass media, which is perhaps why the media and advertising have joined to a strategic alliance where one enables the other. Neither advertising nor the media have control over who they address as anyone and everyone might be spoken to. They cannot know who they speak to because they are unable to receive a response. This failure to communicate does not lie in the nature of advertising or media but in the choice and administering of technology and semantic content. Technology, in the eyes of the market, has the objective to optimise production and productivity. On the one hand, this is achieved in the production process, and on the other hand, in the marketing process. The instrumentalisation and intention behind the use of technology is what disables the advertising complex to respond to a paradigm which would call for intellectual growth, that is, growth not exclusively in productive material terms but also in terms of generation. By designing overdetermined exposures to the world following the paradigm of functional exchangeability of consumers and controlling the circulation of these exposures, it forecloses many possibilities for true generative growth, the growth every generation must begin anew to project without relying on the previous generation. Corporations (within and without the advertising complex) are designed for eternity—not the eternity referred to as all time until the end of the world, but an eternity that defies the natural lifecycles of those irreplaceable singularities who make up the corporation. Consequently, the economic sector knows offspring only as a horizontal or vertical extension of dominance.

If the advertising complex is unable to face singularities, what follows is that it cannot take responsibility for its actions and does not know how to handle the aporias inherent in a singular, human life: responsibility, giving, hospitality. Derrida's ethical gift, in contrast to Bataille's gift of exuberance, requires non-intention and non-recognition. If we are to consider communication as a gift in Derrida's sense, we cannot find an adequate expression for it in today's practice of advertising where visibility is the currency. We cannot find an adequate expression of this gift anywhere, it may be argued, but corporations with the help of the advertising circus go so far as to *make visibility the condition for the gift*. The difference, it seems, is that singularities, at least human singularities, seem to be able to consider or intuit these aporias.

At this point, there should be made a distinction between advertising media that address people irrespective of their own decision to be addressed and advertising media that are consumed by virtue of a series of decisions. The former may be called more honest as they do not convey something they are not and are not reduced to a coextensive role of something else the consumers are really interested in—assuming that most people are not exclusively interested in advertising but ask for an added value for being exposed to it. This however poses a problem for the notion of hospitality. Advertising that is unasked for and cannot be avoided demands of those who are exposed to it absolute hospitality, a strange hospitality since the entity who demands it is not a singularity in a biological sense. The mutual exchangeability of advertising and consumers is such that each can be replaced by something else of equal importance, which, on the one hand, may be read as a prerequisite of absolute hospitality and, on the other hand, its very impossibility. Who is addressed in an intentional act is the anonymous other. Thus, advertising is a strange mingling of the conditional and the unconditional, which is why the ethical response, even the impossible ethical response to advertising is so difficult to get at.

What makes this incompatibility with Derrida more difficult is that he always seems to privilege the question of death: death as the ultimate gift; death as the inevitable outcome of absolute hospitality; death as prerequisite of and obstacle to forgiveness. Death is personal and no one else can assume it for us, just like no one can assume life for us. Legal persons may undergo transformations such as joint ventures and spin-offs, but they do not die the unique, timely death of a unique being just like they do not generate generations the way biological beings do. When a company goes bankrupt and stops existing, it is because no other options were available; it is never because the company came to its own natural end due to old age or incurable illness. When there is the will and the resources to save a company, it can always be done. The role advertising plays in rescuing a company is ambiguous: though it may boost the sales or solidify or communicate a brand image which should further the confidence in the company and thus the sales, it may also lead to overkill. When too much money is spent on outdoing one's opponent before the eyes of the public, this may lead to the exorbitant gift and countergift which could end up in Bataille's ultimate gift: death not due to giving but due to returning too much. Furthermore, better visibility of a company or a product may prove detrimental when a crisis turns up, as was the case with ExxonMobil (or Esso) after the average of Exxon Valdez.

The exchangeability of functionaries within the multi-bodied company and the lack of a fast-forward to one's own death, the lack of empathy, deprive the company of a sense of responsibility. Although it is true that many companies have mission statements and a self-image that incorporates responsibility (corporate social responsibility, CSR), this responsibility does not amount to the same as that taken by singular persons.

How are we, irreplaceable singularities, to face the occupation of our mental sphere by immortal multi-headed entities exposed to the world by the advertising complex? How do we avoid being turned into those immortal but replaceable beings by being addressed by them? How are those multi-headed entities to act upon the challenge of not being mortal and thus not being able to come to rest—keeping in mind that Žižek claims in *The Pervert's Guide to Cinema* that the truly horrible thing is not to be mortal; it is to be immortal.

After all that has been said, one entry point to get to these questions is as intuitive in its conception as it is in its practice. The God-like immortality of corporations and the advertising complex as the entity representing them before the public needs to overcome the danger of hubris and thus the danger of a fatal retribution. More humbleness or modesty is required to face the problem of immortality, an attitude which would also result in a decrease of leakage. How can a new shampoo possibly be of interest to every citizen and every consumer? How are we, along with the advertising complex, to come to a mindset of humbleness? The first insight is the seeming incompatibility between mortals and immortals which then brings us to the awareness of the world, the one and only world, as an interconnected system where every act results in a series of consequences and is thus the beginning of a new future, and where every node, be it biological or intellectual, is connected in some way to all other nodes—from synapses to the cosmos. The basis of all there is is *zoé*: the fact of being cast into this world and having a life to fight for, a life which is only possible and desirable within and among the multitude of other beings; a life for the sake of life and of enabling future life.

The second lesson to learn is the danger of instrumentalised technology and the conditional use of it. Instrumentalisation and conditionality attempt to foresee a future that cannot be foreseen and only in relation to who projects it. It runs the danger of finding a specific measure that eclipses the interrelatedness of other life in order to reduce the unforeseeable future to something that can be grasped and turned into profit. Technology must be internalised as something which enables life, which in itself is boundless and everywhere and cannot be occupied. What we can design is something like a genetic algorithm. We can ask questions of materials like John Cage did, release these questions or algorithms into the world and see what they do, how they absorb their environment. If we do not like the answer, then we ask another question.

Freeing technology to let it fulfil its own destiny requires an attitude of *Gelassenheit*, of equanimity or letting-go. Such Gelassenheit requires a leap of faith and a mindset that allows for fading away as well as letting fade away. Like the brain that is a plastic entity shaping itself and (by secondary operation) others, Gelassenheit means to let go of oneself as well as of others, in order to acquire the ability to be reappropriated again. Without a sense of letting go, one will forever remain blind to one's environment. The difficulty is to draw a line between *Gelassenheit* and *verrohte Gelassenheit* (raw, vulgarised Gelassenheit), as Schirmacher calls it.[408] The former may be likened to peace of mind, a sense of having found one's place in the world, while the latter refers to indifference or disinterest and is characterised by a sensation of "it does not matter anyway" or "I can't do anything about it anyway". The question of letting-go is of equal importance to the advertising complex who creates messages as well as those that are addressed by them. Without a feeling of equanimity, one risks being appropriated and occupied to such a degree that it makes one infertile and incapable to generate.

Gelassenheit allows us to face the aporias of *bios*, of a life in culture. It teaches us to endure the everlasting search for balance, the impossibility of the ethical answer, the impossibility of solution—while still being sensitive to the opposing forces. It teaches us to defer the answer, not in order to get rid of it but in order to pay justice to the interrelatedness of forces. Gelassenheit may also mean a retreat, and this is another point that can be difficult to defend. To retreat may be the only possible means to find peace of mind but there is always the danger that such a movement is a mere flight and does not change what must be changed. A life of retreat becomes a life of flight as there will always be something to retreat from—just like a life of pure forming may become a life of fight, as there will always be something to fight for. In the case of advertising, it appears that the occasional retreat of those who advertise would not only serve their credibility but that of the whole advertising industry. When someone or something is always present it is taken for granted and flexibility asks us to accept it. This is a great obstacle to rupture which would enable invention and generation.

---

408   Schirmacher, Ereignis Technik, 57.

The last possible point of rupture is where there is no more sustainability: the point where more is extracted than given back; where more mental and other material space is extracted than given back. Although everything is a back-and-forth, always dodging the point of balance, what we must be aware of is the point where an asymmetry increases to such a degree that it gains its own momentum. Whenever it gains too much momentum, the counter-movement will be all the more violent to dissipate what was extracted unduly, or it will retreat into indifference and resignation.

For lack of better knowledge, indifference to advertising is met today, and presumably in the past too, by the advertising complex with more and louder advertising. In the case of those who are addressed by advertising and have become immune to it, it would be desirable that they retreated a little less often; that some of the Gelassenheit which has turned into indifference is left behind in order to get to the rupture and prevent the barrier of indifference to be continuously set higher following Bataille's ever-revolving spiral of the countergift. The lack of sensory organs of multi-head-ed organisations and of communication designed particularly as one-way communication carries the risk to get run over due to the inability to perceive danger. This is what happened with the outdoor advertising industry in São Paulo and it is also what hap-pened with Vardan Kushnir, a Russian large-scale spammer who was found murdered in his apartment on 25 July 2005.

It seems that the brain teaches us a responsibility to respond and not only succumb to the flexibility required by one-way, top-down communication hierarchies at work in advertising. If the plasticity of the brain is such that it opens the space for self-for-mation but simultaneously for the formation of our environment, for being formed and for forming, it would be a defeat to retreat into the flexibility of being formed. We have a respons-ability, the capacity to respond or not to respond, even though we concede that every sensible question is already a response and every response is itself the opening of an unknown future, the posing of another question. The response of responsibility is not only an expression of being formed but of forming, of shaping the world and assuming accountability for it. We are our synapses.

Acknowledgments

Many are involved before a book like this one makes it to the printing press. First, I want to say thank you to all those people who have sharpened my understanding of the world. I am particularly indebted to David Cook who first introduced me to this kind of thinking and Marcel Danesi who made it possible for me to receive this introduction at the University of Toronto. I would not have arrived at the point I am today without the intellectual gifts so readily given by many of my professors at the European Graduate School. I would like to name a selected few—in alphabetical order: Alain Badiou, Manuel DeLanda, Martin Hielscher, Jean-Luc Nancy, Avital Ronell, Wolfgang Schirmacher, Michael Schmitt, Sandy Stone, Fred Ulfers, Paul Virilio, Slavoj Žižek. Equally important were many of my fellow students, some of whom I was able to offer hospitality. A very special thanks goes to Erich Hörl, who, in one evening at my dwelling in Zurich, more or less inadvertently pointed me to sources that ended up shaping the argument considerably.

I am also indebted to many unnamed people whose unreflected and anti-intellectual dealings with advertising showed me the necessity of such a book. All those people and things that made me understand that I cannot offer them hospitality anymore were of crucial importance for this book.

The other group of people that have enabled this book are those who closely read it at all stages of composition. Karin Schraner was always my first and sometimes my second reader. She also gave the German translation a close read, which in turn influenced the English version again. Most of all she deserves my eternal gratitude for accepting and supporting me in my ways and living her life at my side. Will Sims also deserves my gratitude for giving the dissertation two close reads and contesting some of my arguments, especially with regards to advertising and our understanding of living in a natural world. Martin Hielscher read the first and last chapter when I felt insecure about the validity of the work and gave me his blessings. Mark Cohen took the time to read the entire dissertation and write an evaluation for the defense committee. Marnie Dibisch was so kind as to do a last spell-check of the final version in this layout. Many thanks to her too.

Lastly, there are people to thank whose support enabled me to attend the European Graduate School. Even though my parents had little understanding of what I was experiencing there, they backed me up financially when I was unable to. My employer not only secured a pay-day, he also gave me time off to write the dissertation.

Bibliography

This book was written in Switzerland. Many source were therefore not available in English language. Page numbers in the footnotes refer to the title quoted in the footnote. URLs were last checked on 20 Nov 2008.

Agamben, G. *Homo Sacer. Die souveräne Macht und das nackte Leben.* Frankfurt: Edition Suhrkamp, 2002. Trans. *Homo Sacer: Sovereign Power and Bare Life.* Stanford, CA: Stanford University Press, 1998.

———. *Ausnahmezustand.* Frankfurt: Suhrkamp, 2004.

———. *Mittel ohne Zweck.* Zürich-Berlin: Diaphanes, 2001.

Anders, G. *Die Antiquiertheit des Menschen, Band I.* München: C.H. Beck, 1956.

———. *Die Antiquiertheit des Menschen, Band II.* München: C.H. Beck, 1980.

Anholt, S. *Brand New Justice : The Upside of Global Branding.* Oxford: Butterworth-Heinemann, 2003.

APG Plakatforschung Schweiz. *APGTraffic: Fallbeispiel Transport publics de la region lausannoise,* 2007.

Arena, G, Riggio, A, Visocchi, P (Eds.). *Monastero e castello nella costruzione del paesaggio.* Perugia: RUX Editrice, 2000.

Arendt, H. *Vita activa oder Vom tätigen Leben.* München: Piper, 2002.

———. *The Portable Hannah Arendt* (Ed. Peter Baehr). New York,

NY: Penguin, 2000.

———. *Eichmann in Jerusalem*. München-Zürich: Piper, 2006.

Arreguín-Toft, I. *How the Weak Win Wars: A Theory of Asymmetric Conflict*. Cambridge, UK: Cambridge University Press, 2005.

Badiou, A. *Das Jahrhundert*. Zürich-Berlin: Diaphanes, 2006.

———. *Wofür steht der Name Sarkozy?* Zürich-Berlin: Diaphanes, 2008.

———. *Kleines Handbuch der In-Ästhetik*. Wien: Turia + Kant, 2001.

Badiou, A & Žižek, S. *Philosophie und Aktualität*. Wien: Passagen, 2005.

Banksy. *Wall and Piece*. London: Century, 2005.

Barthes, R. *Camera Lucida*. New York, NY: Hill and Wang, 1982.

———. *Image—Music—Text*. New York, NY: Hill and Wang, 1977.

———. *Mythen des Alltags*. Frankfurt: Suhrkamp, 1964. Trans. *Mythologies*, Lavers, A (Ed.), London: Jonathan Cape, 1972.

———. *The Grain of the Voice*. Berkley, CA: University of California Press, 1991.

Bataille, G. *The Accursed Share, Volume I*. New York, NY: Zone Books, 1989.

———. *Das obszöne Werk*. Reinbek bei Hamburg: Rowohlt, 2002.

———. *Das Blau des Himmels*. Danzig: Verlag "Freiheit für Polen", 1982.

Baudrillard, J. *Screened Out*. New York, NY: Verso, 2002.

———. *Amerika*. München: Matthes & Seitz, 1987.

———. *Die Illusion des Endes*. Berlin: Merve, 1994.

———. *The Spirit of Terrorism*. New York, NY: Verso, 2002.

———. "The Violence of the Image and the Violence Done to the Image."

Beck, U (Ed.). *Kinder der Freiheit*. Frankfurt: Suhrkamp, 1997.

Benjamin, W. *Das Kunstwerk im Zeitalter seiner technischen Reproduzierbarkeit*. Frankfurt: Suhrkamp, 1963.

———. *Illuminations*. Arendt H (Ed.). New York, NY: Harcourt, Brace & World, 1968.

———. *Zur Kritik der Gewalt und andere Aufsätze*. Frankfurt: Suhrkamp, 1965.

Berger, A A. *Ads, Fads, and Consumer Culture: Advertising's Impact on American Character and Society*. Lanham, ML: Rowman & Littlefield Publishers, 2000.

Blanchot, M. *Die Literatur und das Recht auf den Tod*. Berlin: Merve, 1982.

Blask, F. *Jean Baudrillard zur Einführung*. Hamburg: Junius, 2005.

Braungart, M & McDonough, W. *Einfach intelligent produzieren*. Berlin: Berliner Taschenbuch Verlag, 2005.

Breton, A. *L'amour fou*. Frankfurt: Suhrkamp, 1994.

Buber, M. *I and Thou*. New York, NY: Touchstone Books, 1996.

Butler, J. "On Jacques Derrida". *London Review of Books*. Vol. 26:21. London, 2004.

———. *Precarious life: the powers of mourning and violence*. New York, NY: Verso, 2004.

———. *Antigone's Claim: kinship between life and death*. New York, NY: Columbia University Press, 2000.

Cage, J. Empty Words: Writings '73–'78. Middletown, CT: Wesleyan University Press, 1979.

De Certeau, M. *The Practice of Everyday Life*. Berkley, CA: University of California Press, 1984.

De Landa, M. *War in the Age of Intelligent Machines*. New York, NY: Zone Books, 1991.

Deleuze, G & Guattari, F. *Rhizom*. Berlin: Merve, 1977.

Deleuze, G. *Die Falte: Leibniz und der Barock*. Frankfurt: Suhrkamp, 2000. Trans. The Fold: Leibniz and the Baroque. Minneapolis, MN: University of Minnesota Press, 1992.

Dempf, R (Ed.). *Delete! Die Entschriftung des öffentlichen Raums.*
Wien: Orange-Press, 2006.

Derrida, J. *Of Hospitality.* Stanford, CA: Stanford University
Press, 2000.

———. *On Cosmopolitanism and Forgiveness.* New York, NY:
Routledge, 1997.

———. *Die Einsprachigkeit des Anderen.* München: Wilhelm Fink,
2003.

———. *The Politics of Friendship.* London: Verso, 2005. Trans.
Politik der Freundschaft. Frankfurt: Suhrkamp, 2002.

———. *Given Time: I. Counterfeit Money.* Chicago, IL: The
University of Chicago Press, 1992.

———. *The Gift of Death.* Chicago, IL: The University of Chicago
Press, 1995.

———. "LIMITED INC a b c ..." In: *Limited Inc.* Wien: Passagen
Verlag, 2001.

Derrida, J & Blanchot, M. *Ein Zeuge von jeher / Der Augenblick
meines Todes.* Berlin: Merve, 2003.

Derrida, J & de Montaigne, M. *Über die Freundschaft.* Frankfurt:
Suhrkamp, 2000.

Dery, M. *Escape Velocity.* New York, NY: Grove Press, 1996.

———. *Culture Jamming: Hacking, Slashing and Sniping
in the Empire of Signs.* http://www.markdery.
com/archives/books/culture_jamming

Diprose, R. "Responsibility in a Place and Time of Terror." in:
Borderlands e-Journal, Vol 3. No 1, 2004.

Eco, U. *Zeichen. Einführung in einen Begriff und seine Geschichte.*
Frankfurt: Suhrkamp, 1977.

Felser, G. *Werbe- und Konsumentenpsychologie.* Heidelberg/
Berlin/Oxford: Spektrum Akademischer Verlag, 1997.

Ferris, D S (Ed.). *Walter Benjamin: Theoretical Questions.*
Stanford, CA: Stanford University Press, 1996.

Fløistad, G. "Leibniz: den preetablerte harmoni", in: *Filosofi og vitenskap fra renessansen til vår egen tid*. Oslo: Universitetsforlaget, 1983.

Flusser, V. *Medienkultur*. Frankfurt: Fischer, 1997.

Foucault, M. *Discipline & Punish: The Birth of the Prison*. New York, NY: Vintage, 1995.

———. *The History of Sexuality, Vol. 1: An Introduction*. New York, NY: Vintage, 1978.

———. "Space, Power and Knowledge". In *The Cultural Studies Reader* edited by Simon During, New York, NY: Routledge, 1999.

———. *The Essential Foucault*, Rabinow P & Rose N (Eds.). New York, NY: The New Press, 2003.

Frances, S. *Becoming Secure: Addressing the Aporia Between in(Security)*. Dissertation at the European Graduate School, Saas Fee. 2006.

Freud, S. *Zwei Fallberichte*. Frankfurt: Fischer, 1997.

Gaare, J & Sjaastad, Ø. *Pippi og Sokrates. Filosofiske vandringer i Astrid Lindgrens verden*. C. Huitfeldt Forlag, 2000.

Gadamer, H-G. *Wer bin Ich und wer bist Du*. Frankfurt: Suhrkamp, 1973.

Gordon, H. *The Heidegger-Buber Controversy: The Status of the I-Thou*. Westport, CT: Greenwood Press, 2001.

Gore, A. *Wege zum Gleichgewicht*. Frankfurt: Fischer, 1992. Trans. *Earth in the Balance: Ecology and the Human Spirit*. Boston, MA: Rodale Books, 1992.

Gossage, H L. *Ist die Werbung noch zu retten?* Düsseldorf: Econ, 1967.

———. *The Book of Gossage*. Chicago, IL: The Copy Workshop, 2006.

Hänggi, C. *Out-of-home advertising in the twenty-first century:*

the sell-out of public space? Master thesis at the University
of Lugano, Switzerland: 2003.

Haraway, D. *Simians, Cyborgs, and Women: The Reinvention of
Nature.* London: Routledge, 1991.

Heidegger, M. "Die Frage nach der Technik." In: *Gesamtausgabe
Band 7.* Frankfurt: Vittorio Klostermann, 2000.

———. *Basic Writings.* San Francisco, CA: Harper, 1993.

———. *Der Begriff der Zeit.* Tübingen: Max Niemeyer Verlag, 1995.

———. *Sein und Zeit.* Tübingen: Max Niemeyer Verlag, 2006.

Johnson, S. *Emergence. The connected lives of ants, brains, cities
and software.* London: Penguin, 2002.

Jonas, H. "Prinzip Verantwortung – Zur Grundlegung einer
Zukunftsethik." In *Naturethik*, Krebs, A (Ed.). Frankfurt:
Suhrkamp, 1997.

Klein, N. *No Logo.* London, UK: Flamingo, 2000.

Lasn, K. *Culture Jam: How to reverse America's Suicidal Consumer
Binge—And why we must.* New York, NY: HarperCollins
Publishers Inc., 1999.

Latour, B & Weibel, P (Eds.). *Making Things Public: Atmospheres
of Democracy.* Cambridge, MA: The MIT Press, 2005.

Leibniz, G W. *Monadologie.* Wien: Braumüller und Seidel,
1847. Trans. "The Principles of Philosophy, or, The
Monadology". In: Ariew, R and Watkins, E. *Readings in
Modern Philosophy, Volume I: Descartes, Spinoza, Leibniz
and Associated Texts.* Hackett Pub Co Inc, 2000.

Lesch, W. "Fragmente einer Theorie der Gerechtigkeit:
Emmanuel Levinas im Kontext zeitgenössischer Versuche
einer Fundamentalethik (Habermas, Lyotard, Derrida)",
in: Klehr, F J. (Ed.) *Den andern denken—Philosophisches
Fachgespräch mit Emmanuel Levinas.* Stuttgart: Akademie
der Diözese Rottenburg-Stuttgart, 1991.

Lessig, L. *Free Culture.* New York, NY: The Penguin Press, 2004.

Lessing, T. *Nietzsche.* München: Matthes & Seitz, 1985.

Levinas, E. "Sterben für...: Zum Begriff der Eigentlichkeit bei Martin Heidegger", in: Klehr, F J (Ed.). *Den andern denken—Philosophisches Fachgespräch mit Emmanuel Levinas.* Stuttgart: Akademie der Diözese Rottenburg-Stuttgart, 1991.

Lindgren, A. *Pippi Langstrumpf.* Hamburg: Verlag Friedrich Oetinger, 1984.

Lyotard, J-F. *Das postmoderne Wissen.* Wien: Passagen, 1999.

Malabou, C. *Was tun mit unserem Gehirn?* Zürich-Berlin: Diaphanes, 2006.

Mandel E & Taras D (Eds.). *A Passion for Identity: An Introduction to Canadian Studies.* Toronto: Methuen, 1987.

Mauss, M. *The Gift.* London: Routledge, 1990.

McLuhan, M. *Understanding Media.* Cambridge, MA: The MIT Press, 1964.

McLuhan, M, Fiore, Q & Agel, A. *The Medium is the Massage.* Corte Madera CA: Gingko Press, 2001.

McLuhan, M & Powers, B R. *The Global Village: Transformations in World Life and Media in the 21ˢᵗ Century.* New York, NY: Oxford University Press, 1989.

Miller, A. *Death of a Salesman.* London: Penguin, 1976.

Miller, P D. *Rhythm Science.* Cambridge, MA: The MIT Press, 2004.

Nancy, J-L. *Singulär plural sein.* Berlin: Diaphanes, 2004.

——. *Corpus.* Berlin: Diaphanes, 2003.

——. *L'intrus.* East Lansing, MI: Michigan State University Press, 2002.

——. "Corpus", in: *Thinking Bodies.* MacCannell, J F & Zakarin, L (Eds.). Stanford, CA: Stanford University Press, 1994.

Nietzsche, F. *Jenseits von Gut und Böse.* München: Goldmann, 1999.

——. *Also sprach Zarathustra.* Essen: Phaidon.

——. *The Gay Science.* Cambridge: Cambridge University Press,

2001.

———. *Die Geburt der Tragödie*. Frankfurt: Insel Verlag, 1994.

———. *Ecce Homo*. München: C.H.Beck, 2005.

———. *Werke 1 & 2*. Stuttgart: Alfred Kröner Verlag, 1938.

———. *The Will to Power*. New York, NY: Random House, 1968.

Ogilvy, D. *Über Werbung*. Düsseldorf / Wien: Econ, 1984.

Pamuk, O. *Der Blick aus meinem Fenster: Betrachtungen*. Frankfurt: Fischer, 2008.

Pynchon, T. *The Crying of Lot 49*. New York, NY: Perennial, 1965.

———. "Mortality and Mercy in Vienna". In: *Epoch* (Cornell University). Spring 1959, Vol IX, No. 4. Online version: http://www.themodernword.com/pynchon/ pynchon_mortality.html

Quart, A. *Branded*. München: Riemann Verlag, 2003.

Ronell, A. *The Test Drive*. Urbana and Chicago, IL: University of Illinois Press, 2005.

———. *Stupidity*. Urbana and Chicago, IL: University of Illinois Press, 2002.

Saramago, J. *The Cave*. London: Harcourt, 2003.

Schirmacher, W. *Ereignis Technik*. Wien: Passagen-Verlag, 1990.

———. "Homo Generator in Artificial Life: From a Conversation with Jean-François Lyotard." In: *Poiesis*. Vol. 7. Toronto: EGS Press, 2005.

———. "What if?: A Tribute to Jacques Derrida." In: *Poiesis*. Vol. 7. Toronto: EGS Press, 2005.

———. "From the Phenomenon to the Event of Technology: A Dialectical Approach to Heidegger's Phenomenology." In: Durbin F & Rapp F (Eds.). *Philosophy and Technology. Boston Studies in the Philosophy of Science 80*. Dordrecht; Kluwer Academic Publishers. 1983

———. "Eco-Sofia: The Artist of Life." In: *Ethics and Technology* (Ed. Carl Mitcham). Greenwich, 1989.

———. "Ethik im Horizont der Künstlichkeit." In: Margreiter, R and Leidlmair, K (Eds.) *Heidegger (Technik – Ethik – Politik)* Würzburg: Königshausen & Neumann, 1991.

———. "Homo Generator: Media and Postmodern Technology." In: Bender, G & Duckrey T (Eds.). *Culture on the Brink: Ideologies of Technology.* New York, NY: The New Press, 1994/1999.

———. "Net Culture". In: *Poiesis 3.* EGS Press. Toronto, 2001.

———. "Homo Generator: Die Provokation der Gen-Technologie". Innsbruck, 1986.

Schirmacher, W (Ed). *German 20th Century Philosophical Writings.* New York-London: Continuum, 2003.

Sebeok, T A. *Global Semiotics.* Bloomington, IN: Indiana University Press: 2001.

Siegenthaler, C P. *Ökobilanz – 30 Jahre Forschung an der Schnittstelle zwischen Natur- und Wirtschaftswissenschaften.* Dissertation at the University of St. Gallen (HSG), Switzerland.

Starr, T & Hayman, E. *Signs and Wonders: The Spectacular Marketing of America.* New York: Doubleday, 1998.

Stiglitz, J E. *Economics of the Public Sector.* New York, NY: W. W. Norton, 2000.

Stone, A R. *The War of Desire and Technology at the Close of the Mechanical Age.* Cambridge, MA: The MIT Press, 1995.

Topf, J. *Antispam-Strategien: unerwünschte E-Mails erkennen und abwehren.* Köln: Bundesanzeiger Verlag, 2005.

Twitchell, J B. *Adcult USA: The Triumph of Advertising in American Culture.* New York, NY: Columbia University Press, 1999.

Ulmer, G L. *Heuretics: The logic of invention.* Baltimore, MD: The John Hopkins University Press, 1994.

———. *Teletheory.* New York-Hamburg: Atropos, 2004.

Virilio, P. *Open Sky.* London-New York: Verso, 1997.

———. *Krieg und Fernsehen.* Frankfurt: Fischer, 1997.

———. *Ground Zero.* London-New York: Verso, 2002.

———. *Die Eroberung des Körpers.* Frankfurt: Fischer, 1996.

———. *Revolutionen der Geschwindigkeit.* Berlin: Merve, 1993.

———. *Ereignislandschaft.* München/Wien: Hanser, 1998.

Venturi, R, Scott Brown, D, Izenour, S. *Learning from Las Vegas.* Cambridge, MA: The MIT Press, 2001.

Watzlawick, P, Beavin J H, Jackson, D D. *Menschliche Kommunikation.* Bern: Verlag Hans Huber, 1982.

Weber, S. *Targets of opportunity: on the militarization of thinking.* New York, NY: Fordham University Press, 2005.

Wilke, J (Ed). *Zum Naturbegriff der Gegenwart, Band 1.* Stuttgart: Frommann Holzboog, 2001.

Žižek, S. *Die Revolution steht bevor: Dreizehn Versuche über Lenin.* Frankfurt: Suhrkamp, 2002.

Zylinska, J (Ed). *The Cyborg Experiments: The extensions of the body in the media age.* New York, NY: Continuum, 2002.

Newspaper, journal and magazine articles

BBC News, "Legal case against God dismissed". 16 Oct 2008.

Biotechnology and Biological Sciences Research Council, "Waggle dance controversy resolved by radar records of bee flight paths", 11 May 2005.

Binswanger, D. "Rechter Haken". *Weltwoche* 02/2005. Zürich

———. "Radikal, pauschal, scheissegal". *Weltwoche* 41/2005. Zürich.

———. "Denkerin vor dem Herrn". *Weltwoche* 25/2006. Zürich.

"Das Stadtbild São Paulos wird gesäubert". *Neue Zürcher Zeitung,* 12 Feb 2007. Zürich.

Falkai, P. "Braing-imaging: Faszinierende Forschungen verändern Psychiatrie nachhaltig". *Informationsdienst Wissenschaft,* 20 Nov 2003.

Fetzer, F. "Zahlen, bitte". *Weltwoche* 37/2006. Zürich.

Gächter, S. "Jean-François Lyotard und Jacques Derrida: Totalität in Fetzen". *Du*, Nr. 11 / Nov 1991.

Genner, S. "'Züri malt' – Wirbel um weisse Werbeplakate". Zürich: *iQ* 49/2005.

Hänggi, C. "Wildwuchs im Werbewald". *iQ* 43/2004, Zürich.

———. "WC-Werbung wider Willen". *re:flex*. Nr. 8, 04/2005, Zürich.

Hayden, A. "Advertising and the end of history". Toronto: *Stay Free! Magazine*, Vol. 35 issue 4.

Kalberer, G. "In der Logik lauert das Totalitäre". *Tages-Anzeiger*, Zürich, 11 Oct 2004.

Köhler, A. "Stilistin des genauen Blicks: Zum Tod der Schriftstellerin und Essayistin Susan Sontag". *Neue Zürcher Zeitung*, Zürich. 30 Dec 2004.

Kohler, G. "Freiheit, Gleichheit und die liberale Philosophie". *Neue Zürcher Zeitung*, Zürich. 12/13 Nov 2005.

Kuhn, A. "Interview mit einem schnellen Brüter". *Weltwoche* 45/2005, Zürich.

Lüönd, K. "Bis zur Bewusstlosigkeit?" *Werbewoche*, Zürich, 15 Nov 2006.

Marquard, O. "Hans Blumenberg: Entlastung vom Absoluten", in *Das Verschwinden der Wirklichkeit. Ein Kursbuch. Du*, Nr. 11 / Nov 1991.

Meyer, M. "Hannah Arendt, die Leidenschaft des Denkens." *Neue Zürcher Zeitung*, Zürich. 14/15 Oct 2006.

———. "Die Wahrheit ist Kunst – Oder: Nietzsches Ästhetisierung der Welt." *Neue Zürcher Zeitung*, Zürich. 4/5 Dec 2004.

Moser, H. "Die Stadt hinter Reklametafeln hervorgeholt". *Tages-Anzeiger*, 24 May 2007. Zürich.

Muschg, A. "Schule Europa". *Neue Zürcher Zeitung*, Zürich. 14/15 April 2007.

Murdoch, R. "Universum der Inhalte". *Persönlich*, Rapperswil.

April 2004.

Rohter, L. "Streets Are Paved With Neon's Glare, and City Calls a Halt". *New York Times*, 12 Dec 2006, New York.

Schlüter, C. "Die Falte zwischen Leib und Seele". *DIE ZEIT* 47/1995.

Sontag, S. "Regarding the Torture of Others". *New York Times Magazine*, 23 May 2004, New York.

Ulrich, P. "Bürgerfreiheit und zivilisierte Marktwirtschaft". *Neue Zürcher Zeitung*, Zürich. 19 Oct 2005.

Weder, M. "Der Tod des Anderen ist der erste Tod". *Tages-Anzeiger*, Zürich. 12 Jan 2006.

Wenzel, U J. "Glauben schenken, Stimme leihen: Zum Tod des französischen Philosophen Jacques Derrida." *Neue Zürcher Zeitung*, Zürich. 11 Oct 2004.

Žižek, S. "Ein Nein der Hoffnung". *DIE ZEIT*, Hamburg. 9 June 2005.

Electronic resources and references

Allianz gegen Werbeverbote. http://www.stopp-werbeverbote.ch.

Collection of lectures from the European Graduate School on Youtube (Badiou, Baudrillard, Butler, DeLanda, Derrida, Ronell, Virilio, Žižek *et al.*) http://www.youtube.com/profile?user=egsvideo.

European Graduate School. http://www.egs.edu.

Hänggi, C. "Violent new media". Blog entry for the course *Network, Knowledge and the Digital Age* at the University of Prince Edward Island, Charlottetown. 10 Nov 2004. Now hosted at http://www.markhemphill.com/pippi.

IAA Global (International Advertising Association). http://www.iaaglobal.org.

IG Plakat | Raum | Gesellschaft. http://www.plakat-raum-gesellschaft.ch.

LaVey, A S. "The Eleven Satanic Rules of the Earth". Excerpt from

the *Satanic Bible*, 1967. http://www.churchofsatan.com/
Pages/Eleven.html.

MELANI – Melde- und Analysestelle Informationssicherung.
http://www.melani.admin.ch.

Nietzsche, F. *Thus spoke Zarathustra*. Translation by Thomas
Common, edited by Paul Douglas.
http://users.telenet.be/sterf/texts/phil/Nietzsche-
ThusSpokeZarathustra.pdf.

Persoenlich.com. http://www.persoenlich.com

Redefining Progress: The Nature of Economics.
http://www.rprogress.org.

Schweizer Werbung SW. http://www.sw-ps.ch .

Sihlcity. http://www.sihlcity.ch .

Symantec Internet Security Threat Report. http://www.symantec.
com

TV Ontario, "Marshall McLuhan's ABC", 3 Dec 2002, 21h.

Universal Declaration of Human Rights. http://www.un.org/
Overview/rights.html.

Werbewoche. http://www.werbewoche.ch.

World Federation of Advertisers. http://www.wfanet.org.

Žižek, S. The Pervert's Guide to Cinema, DVD, 2006.

Encyclopaedias and dictionaries

Das grosse Kunstlexikon von P. W. Hartmann, http://www.beyars.
com/kunstlexikon

Dictionary of Sociology, Marshall, G (Ed.). Oxford University
Press, 1998.

Dictionary of the Social Sciences. Calhoun, C(Ed.). Oxford
University Press, 2002.

The Internet Encyclopedia of Philosophy. Dowden, B & Fieser, J
(Eds.). http://www.utm.edu/research/iep/

Duden Fremdwörterbuch, 5. Auflage. Mannheim/Wien/Zürich: Dudenverlag, 1990.

Georges, Lateinisch-Deutsches Wörterbuch Bd. 1, 1967.

The Oxford Companion to Philosophy. Hondering, T. (Ed.). Oxford: Oxford University Press, 1995.

Philosophielexikon. Hügli, A & Lübcke, P (Eds.). Reinbek bei Hamburg: Rowohlt, 2003.

KLUGE *Etymologisches Wörterbuch der deutschen Sprache,* 24. Auflage. Berlin/New York: Walter de Gruyter, 2002.

Langenscheidt Schulwörterbuch Latein. Berlin/München: Langenscheidt, 1997.

Le Micro-Robert. Paris: Dictionnaires Le Robert, 1992.

LEO *Online dictionary English/German and French/German.* http://dict.leo.org

Lexikon der Nachhaltigkeit. http://www.nachhaltigkeit.info

Oxford Advanced Learner's Dictionary. Oxford: Oxford University Press, 1995.

Tysk-Norsk Blå Ordbok. Oslo: Kunnskapsforlaget, 1990.

Think Media: EGS Media Philosophy Series

Wolfgang Schirmacher, editor

The Ethics of Uncertainty: Aporetic Openings. Michael Anker

Trans/actions: Art, Film and Death. Bruce Alistair Barber

Literature as Pure Mediality: Kafka and the Scene of Writing.
Paul DeNicola

Imaginality: Conversant and Eschaton. A. Staley Groves

Hospitality in the age of media representation. by Christian Hänggi

**The Organic Organisation: freedom, creativity and
the search for fulfilment.** Nicholas Ind

Can Computers Create Art? James Morris

**The Art of the Transpersonal Self: Transformation as Aesthetic and
Energetic Practice.** Norbert Koppensteiner

Community without Identity: The Ontology and Politics of Heidegger.
Tony See

Sonic Soma: Sound, Body and the Origins of the Alphabet.
Elise Kermani

Mirrors triptych technology: Remediation and Translation Figures.
Diana Silberman Keller

—— *other books available from Atropos Press*

Teletheory. Gregory L. Ulmer

Philosophy of Culture-Kulturphilosophie: Schopenhauer and Tradition.
Edited by Wolfgang Schirmacher.

Virilio: Grey Ecology. The La Rochelle Workshop.
Edited by Hubertus von Amelunxen. Translated by Drew Burk

The Tupperware Blitzkrieg. Anthony Metivier

Talking Cheddo: Teaching Hard Kushitic Truths. Manga Clem Marshall

Che Guevera and the Economic Debate in Cuba. Luiz Bernardo Pericás

Follow Us or Die. Vincent W.J. van Gerven Oei and Jonas Staal

Just Living: Philosophy in Artificial Life. Collected Works Volume 1.
Wolfgang Schirmacher